1993

The Collaborative Dimensions of Learning

Mary Hamm   Dennis Adams

ABLEX PUBLISHING CORPORATION
NORWOOD, NEW JERSEY

Library of Congress Cataloging-in-Publication Data

Hamm, Mary.
   The collaborative dimensions of learning : cultural diversity &
restructuring schools with cooperative learning across the curriculum
/ Mary Hamm, Dennis Adams.
     p.   cm.
   Includes bibliographical references and index.
   ISBN 0-89391-754-0
   1. Team learning approach in education.   2. Intercultural
education—United States.   I. Adams, Dennis M. II. Title.
LB1032.H358 1991
371.3'95—dc20   91-28440
                                               CIP

Ablex Publishing Corporation
355 Chestnut Street
Norwood, New Jersey 07648

CONTENTS

PREFACE

This book takes a close look at the issues, trends, and practical teaching concerns that surround cooperative learning. It puts forward specific organizational plans and content area lessons for teachers who would like to become more familiar with active team learning in the classroom. Major themes include collaborative approaches to multicultural educational, creativity, literacy, numeracy, educational technology, and an interdisciplinary curriculum. The book is written for teachers, administrators, workshop leaders, curriculum developers, and evaluators. It would also be of interest to parents and political decision makers.

Changing demographics are bringing questions of race and ethnicity to the fore in American education. Pluralism is a positive national value underlying a basic respect for the students' cultural background while supporting a sense of belonging to an American community with common bonds. Pluralistic multiculturalism seeks a richer, more inclusive, common culture. The goal is to teach children that all people—regardless of race, ethnicity, or gender—can achieve their goals in society if they aim high and are tenacious. In doing their part to make this happen, schools must not only attend to children's minds but also to their physical, psychological, and social needs.

The educational reform movement of recent years has only made a few dents in resolving either the multicultural concerns or the educational problems of America. To inquire into these problems requires raising some fundamental questions about our society's prejudices, preferences, and levels of commitment. Unless today's schools are considered in a broader context, the best of educational plans and methods will have little effect. Placing a shiny coat of new paint over tired concepts and techniques will not help us face up to the grim data on the educational competency of young Americans. Many of the problems of our schools are as much spiritual and social as they are technical or instructional. Real change requires a society that *wants* to do something and teachers who know *how* to do it.

Many educators are working to change schools and make provisions for new organization patterns, innovative teaching methods and cultural diversity. This book hopes to provide some practical suggestions that will help this developmental process. Some schools are already welcoming promising developments like cooperative learning, instructional technology, interdisciplinary curricula, and more. But a much greater distance waits to be traveled.

1

ADAPTING COOPERATIVE LEARNING TO THE STUDENTS OF THE 1990s

There is general agreement that robust public schools are essential to our civic health. Yet many companies—from Motorola to General Motors—find that they must spend millions on teaching new workers basic reader, math, problem-solving, and teamwork skills. Little wonder that there is a widespread belief that the American educational system has not been effective in educating a large proportion of its children.

Caught between the absence of secure cultural tradition and a complex (rapidly changing) industrial world, many sections of society are being forced to take a serious look at reforming education. Large businesses, universities, and public and private institutions are beginning to recognize that they have a moral responsibility to help to improve the education of students and teachers (Schorr & Schorr, 1989).

It is becoming apparent sincere reform demands fundamental changes in educational perspective, customs, organizational routine, and classroom structures (Education Commission of the States, 1988). There is general agreement that the very organization of the schools is a problem: excessive bureaucracy and too many top-down regulations. Good schools require an increased teacher influence, community support, and adequate funding.

Trends towards school-based management and restructuring the class-room environment are major planks in school reform efforts. *Cooperative learning* is one of the new structures that has demonstrated its potential for achieving positive results (Slavin, 1986). Cooperative groups are rapidly catching on as a successful learning framework that is making its appearance in school curriculum plans, teacher in service programs, and state guidelines. Whether the issue is equity or developing critical thinking skills, cooperative learning is frequently referred to as a process that works (DeVries & Slavin, 1978).

Cooperative learning challenges the format of ability grouping and teacher-centered instruction. In a cooperative classroom the teacher organizes major parts of the curriculum around tasks, problems, and projects that students can work through in small mixed-ability groups. Teachers design lessons around active learning teams. Students then work together to reach common group goals. Whether its finding out about new concepts, solving problems, or questioning factual information, a collaborative approach has shown that it helps develop academic skills while promoting understanding and self-esteem (Slavin, Sharan, Kagan, Hertz-Lazarowitz, Webb, & Schmuck, 1985). Tapping students' social nature it helps them adjust to the demands of today's workplace and civic culture. When working together in active learning teams, children can combine energies as they reach toward a common goal.

Several years of research and practice suggest that cooperative learning can work to promote active learning (Johnson, Maruyama, Johnson, Nelson, & Skon, 1981). Active problem solving with others has been shown to spark an alertness to mind not achieved in passive listening. When students talk and reason together to complete a task or solve a problem, they become more involved in thinking and communicating (Carnegie Foundation for the Advancement of Teaching, 1986). Although the research and the literature support cooperative learning, the main reason cooperative learning is catching on as a learning technique is that teachers can tell it works.

Language, Learning, and Socialization

Learning includes what's acquired through interaction with the environment, family, community members, schools, and other institutions. Language is the vehicle where meaning is translated, verified, and made conscious. Since learning originates on the social level, social and cultural elements cannot be ignored. By interacting with their environment, parents siblings, and peers, children come to know and make sense of the world (Sharan & Schachar, 1988). This early learning forms an experience base. Later the individual will use language to help clarify connections and build a base for learning.

Cooperative learning builds on the premise that much of learning is social. Collaboration implies giving students opportunities to talk together and participate actively in what's happening in the classroom. Each student brings his or her own interests, learning style, cultural background, and abilities to school. Giving children opportunities to use language as a learning tool gets them more involved, motivated and actively participating

(Shea Bayer, 1990). Students need opportunities to collaborate with peers and adults, to learn and gain expertise, practice, and create. Instead of the teacher being the primary language user, asking questions, lecturing and evaluating, students (in cooperative learning) take center stage as part of the social learning process. The teacher acts as a guide, selecting meaningful topics for discussion, providing opportunities for collaboration, and observing the interaction of peers.

Students are encouraged to make connections between new ideas discussed in class and prior knowledge. In cooperative groups, where students are the primary language users, learning comes alive as meanings are actively constructed. Instead of listening to the teacher talk, interpret, and negotiate meaning, these students have regular opportunities to talk, read, write, and solve problems together as they attempt to construct meaningful explanations.

It has been argued that expressive language is the foundation of student language and thinking (Jager Adams, 1990). To translate this natural process to education, students must be able to struggle with ideas informally before having to shape their thinking and language for a public audience. Groups need time to clarify and expand each other's thinking about a concept. Often starting with their own experiences and background knowledge, this process can move to one of a shared group belief, idea, or opinion.

Unstructured interaction between peers and friends relies heavily on shared experiences for understanding. Much of the talk is expressive, where feelings, beliefs, and opinions are freely stated. Such informal conversations in small groups should not be underestimated. This kind of collaboration and communication is a starting point for coming to terms with new ideas. Through "talking" or "informal bantering" learners shape ideas, modify them by listening to others, question, plan, express doubt and confusion, and construct meaning. In the process they frequently experiment with new language and fee free to express uncertainty.

Talking in mixed-ability groups can facilitate and enhance the learning process (Johnson & Johnson, 1989). Small group discussion allows each individual to become more at ease with sharing thoughts with others. It also helps ideas take shape and become more alive and personal. Expressing ideas helps the group examine, compare, and affix personal meaning to the concepts or beliefs presented. Placing ideas into a personal and collective experience is a powerful motivator, and information tends to be remembered longer because more meaning is attached to it.

Small group discussions can also crate a type of collective consciousness in which all members benefit (Newman & Thompson, 1987). This can provide constant feedback and analysis if the group has a supportive environment and criticizes differing positions in order to *help* one another. The power and diversity of four or five minds is greater than one.

Connecting Today's Students With the Learning Process

The research suggests that, when used appropriately, cooperative learning:

- *Motivates Students*
  Students taking and working together on a project or problem experience the fun and experience of sharing ideas and information.
- *Increases Academic Performance*
  Studies show that classroom interaction with peers causes students—especially those from diverse cultural and linguistic backgrounds—to make significant academic gains, compared with students in tradition settings.
- *Encourages Active Learning*
  Extensive research has shown that students learn more when they're actively engaged in discovery and problems loving.
- *Increases Respect for Diversity*
  Students who work together in mixed ability groups are more likely to select mixed racial and ethnic acquaintances and friendships. When students cooperate to reach a common goal, they learn to appreciate and respect each other.
- *Promotes Literacy and Language Skills*
  Group study offers students many chances to use language and improve speaking skills. This is particularly important for second language students.
- *Helps Prepare Students for Today's Society*
  Team approaches to solving problems, combining energies with others and working to get along are valued skills in the world of work, community, and leisure.
- *Improves Teacher Effectiveness*
  Through actively engaging students in the learning process, teachers also make important discoveries about their students' learning. As peers take responsibility for some of the teaching, the power of the teacher can be multiplied (Slavin, 1988).

Schools today have diverse student populations, with one out of three students living in poverty, according to a 1988 study by The Carnegie Foundation for the Advancement of Teaching. Many of these students miss out on educational advantages from early childhood education to job training. Alienation, poor health care programs, teenage pregnancy, drug abuse, nutrition-related deficiencies, and low self-esteem are common problems. Urban teachers are given little or no support as they face a shocking pattern of problems ranging from parental apathy to disruptive behavior.

In some schools, students are made to feel unwelcome, dumb, uncomfortable, and bored. At the earliest opportunity, many drop out. For students who stay in, schools frequently offer little encouragement to those who have talents extending beyond the ability to manipulate words and numbers. Some youngsters in inner city classrooms have the tough-mindedness ("street smarts") that could assist them in becoming successful leaders and workers. They have learned how to beat the odds and fight the daily battles of personal survival. Many of these students value the cooperation in sports that school teams need to succeed. They know the value of teamwork. What they lack are the academic skills and world knowledge to "make it" in either school or the literacy-intensive workplace. They end up at the bottom of every social, economic, and educational index.

In today's social milieu there is an ever more compelling need for schools to be a socially and intellectually stimulating community of learners. This environment must draw on principles of learning and take into account multiple cultures, languages, and backgrounds of students. Schools can help "at risk" children by creating a caring atmosphere, attending to student interests, promoting meaningful learning, and encouraging acceptance and respect for creative potential. "Personal connectedness," a feeling of belonging, and acceptance by teachers and peers is critical for children of all ages.

Studies show that, when students cooperate to reach a common goal, they learn to appreciate and respect one another (Johnson & Johnson, 1984). For school to be successful, it helps to have students in a community and school culture that values academic achievement and personal commitment. The home environment should not be an excuse for failure. Focusing on poor preparation of disadvantaged children often diverts attention from how poorly the school is prepared to serve these students (Brophy & Good, 1986). Thus students can be placed at a disadvantaged by both the school and the child's environment. They not only come to school poorly prepared, but have schools poorly prepared to help them.

The Educational Mission in a Democratic Society

An important part of the "test" for quality schools is whether they can help children develop analytical abilities, group work skills, and communicative competence across media and disciplines. But this is only part of the story. The mission of an educational system in a democracy must go beyond these basics to helping all of our students develop intellectual talents, civic understanding, a comprehension of humanistic/scientific traditions, and the ability to think critically. With child poverty worsening and the social capital of the family and the community being diminished, this becomes problematic.

Schools frequently avoid the issue and relegate disadvantaged students to lower tracks, where they have the *least* access to the best teachers and an enriched curriculum. Giving these students drill and practice, and avoiding intellectually challenging activity, is at best patroning—at at worst harmful to their long range educational success. Early grouping decisions often become self-fulfilling prophecies, with few minorities in college-bound programs. For the advantaged student, in top ability groups, the emphasis is on critical thinking, creativity, and problem solving—for those at the bottom it's more often basic skills, conformity, and discipline (Cohen, 1986).

Cooperative learning with mixed ability teams offers one alternative to tracking and an emphasis on the basics. It can help students learn to listen, strengthen thinking and improve their leadership skills. Throughout this process it's important that teachers and the curricula be sensitive to the culture and interest of students. If these needs are not met, many students will escape from the negative consequences of "poor academic performance" and seek satisfaction outside of school.

The 1980s were an ostentatious celebration of greed as the wealth of a narrow strata of upper Americans grew by leaps and bounds. Exclusive private schools were in, public school out. Luxury, in education and everything else, became part of American popular culture for those who could afford it, and the ideal for those who couldn't. One wealthy publisher summed up the mood of the decade when he said that his son would "have the best education money can buy...it's tragic about everyone else" (Phillips, 1990).

Many have attributed the country's current educational crisis and sagging productivity to selfishness and lack of discipline (Baida, 1990). Between 1981 and 1989 the net worth of those on the Forbes 400 richest American's list nearly tripled—as did the amount of the nation's wealth shipped overseas. In the 1980s there were also disproportionate rewards for society's legal, economic, and cultural manipulators; while a disproportionate number of female, black, Hispanic, and young Americans lost ground. This happened at the very time urban public schools became gloomy places with peeling paint, broken chairs, and classes in gymnasiums. The quality of the workplace made it very difficult to keep good teachers.

Educational news is bad because most news is bad. We tend to concentrate on the houses burning down rather than on the ones being built. Unfortunately, as far as educational news is concerned, whole blocks are burning. Do we have the social vigor to respond? The political pendulum has swung in the past and is beginning to move again. Educational deprivation is becoming less popular with Americans. The question is will government, business, and the schools take the necessary steps to achieve a cooperate fusion of increasingly diverse elements within our schools and our society?

LIVING IN RELATIONSHIP WITH OTHERS: USING COOPERATIVE GROUPS FOR MULTICULTURAL EDUCATION

One of the central questions of our time is how to live in relationship with others. Whether the effort is made individually or collectively, public reciprocity is often made more difficult by narrow cultural experiences, stereotyped thinking, and certain elements of popular culture. It is hard to calculate or fathom the forces our attitudes and technology are unleashing. From musical lyrics to comedy, multicultural misunderstandings increasing filter into the American consciousness. It's important to examine the soil within which this prejudice is growing. The same intolerance that is now running through today's popular culture runs through today's society. To unify a society that is increasingly divided along racial, cultural, and class lines requires educational structures that accommodate multiple group and personal realities.

Nearly 20 years of research and practice support the use of cooperative groups to focus instruction on the different strengths and styles of students. Evidence of improved academic performance, and of personal and social gains for students of all ages and abilities have been documented (Slavin, 1987; Johnson & Johnson, 1974). An important finding of more recent research is that cooperative learning improves social relations between racially and culturally different students. After working cooperative groups, all members became more accepting of classmates who were different (Webb, 1982; Ziegler, 1981).

Since the basic plan for cooperative learning revolves around the idea of active, small group learning environments, it's a natural vehicle for promoting multicultural understandings. Students at various "ability" levels cluster together, discuss topics, and learn to take charge of their own learning. Sometimes helping behaviors, social skills, and positive interdependence are encouraged by assigning specific roles to group members. At other times group roles like checker, reader encourager, animator, and group leader occur naturally.

Often the teacher needs to set up the problem and help the student team negotiate workable solutions. Once children are familiar with the process the teacher can step back and let them go on their own. Team spirit, rather than individual rivalry, is stressed as students learn to work together to accomplish a learning goal. The objective is not only to complete a task, but to work collectively to help each individual learn.

Interracial learning teams can be useful for organizing classrooms in support of multicultural harmony. These studies from social psychology suggest that dividing the class into interracial learning teams reduces prejudice by undercutting the stereotyped categories while encouraging group members to pull together (Webb, 1982; Ziegler, 1981). Other researchers (like psychologist Spencer Kagan) have found that cooperative groups are particularly beneficial for Hispanic, African-American, and other minority students.

Research on Cooperative Learning

The results of experimental field research on cooperative learning support the following conclusions:

- Cooperative learning improves academic performance among high- and low-achieving students.
- Minority students have made consistently favorable achievement in cooperative classes.
- Disadvantaged students significantly benefit from collaborative learning techniques.
- Working in mixed-ability groups *doesn't stifle* individual initiative.
- Cooperative learning has positive effects on students' self-esteem, social relations, attitudes toward mainstreamed students, and race relations.
- By teaching others, all of the students actually come to understand the material better.
- Children's cooperative behavior skills were shown to transfer to interaction with peers who weren't members of the same learning teams. It also transferred to their behavior in social situations not structured by the teacher.
- Cooperative learning methods have proven to be practical and widely acceptable to teachers.
- When peer value systems take learning seriously, drop-out rates and delinquency levels go down
- The group process seems to assist the development of mature thinkers who are able to cooperate in the acquisition and use of knowledge.
- Cooperative learning methods are often used by teachers to jointly achieve social and academic goals (Slavin, 1983, 1989; Sharan, 1980; Abraham & Campbell, 1984; Levine & Tractman, 1988).

When students are encouraged to work collaboratively, there is a positive effect on the overall school environment. Teachers became more cooperative in their own professional interactions and more willing to collaborate with their peers. Being willing to learn from failure, becoming more attuned to resources, and working beyond personal limits were the attitudes teachers cited most frequently as affecting success with cooperative learning (Slavin et al., 1985) Tenacity is a key to success in just about any field. Just as it is with students, the teachers' commitment to academic and organizational tasks was found to be a major factor in their level of success.

Addressing The Needs of All Students

Generally schools focus on a child's weaknesses rather than strengths—and place students accordingly
    —(Ammon & Ammon, 1987)

We do many students a disservice when we emphasize learning difficulties and group by "ability." The needs of culturally different students may illustrate the less obvious needs of all of our students. Differences should not be confused with defects. A diverse student population presents our schools with many benefits and possibilities for learning about a wide range of cultures. Middle-class students also benefit from a multicultural intellectual life at school—if grouping doesn't prevent them from working directly with multicutural students. Given the demographic trends in the U.S.—and increasing global interdependence—a happy fusion of the diverse groups in American society becomes a real national asset.

The realities of American pluralism would suggest that educators become attuned to the diverse interests of today's students and their parents. Since the money flows where the children of the powerful go to school, separate will never be equal. Keeping the middle-class student in the public schools is as important as educating the children of poverty. Most parents, teachers, and concerned citizens realize that they cannot ignore their responsibility for promoting social justice. In the past this has taken the form of support for equity programs such as multicultural education or bilingual education. Many of these efforts have been helpful. But some have been rather superficial gestures designed to quiet calls for fundamental change.

Multicultural educational programs should not be viewed as sops to minorities. Rather, they are part of a quality education for all children. For programs to work, mainstream members of a society must value multicultural education as a positive factor in a culturally diverse society. The objective is to spark conversations both within and across communities and cultures.

Using Cultural Learning Tools

There may be a troubling revival of cultural intolerance, but covert prejudice is even more insidious. Anyone who works with the schools has to do a great deal of self-examination concerning accidental cultural biases. A teacher might, for example, express less direct or accidental prejudice by an overly negative response to a mistake or by *overpraising* marginally successful work on a project Even with the best of intentions, teachers can undermine a child's self-esteem. Words like *normal, success,* are culturally defined. Even pulling students out of the regular classroom for special treatment programs can backfire unless it is thoughtfully organized.

In order to serve today's population of students, both the curricula and teachers must be involved with the culture, abilities, and lifestyles of the students being served. The most successful teachers know that the good lessons are structured around a child's interests—while making collaborative connections to the real world. Consciousness is never a series of separate categories. That's why most learning experiences, including multicultural ones, work best in a mainstreamed classroom where they permeate the whole curriculum.

A recent study, "The Effects of Migration on Children" (U.S. Government Publications, 1990), suggests that a major reason for the failure to reach minorities is the fact that government policies are oriented towards the beliefs and behavior of the upper middle class. The report addresses these failures and offers some suggestions for addressing cultural differences. Its recommendations include:

1. Creating a system that would pay students (who are most prone to drop out) to stay in school.
2. Establishing high expectations and a school climate that supports learning.
3. Forming an itinerant-teacher program that would send teachers to the homes of some migrant and minority students.
4. Developing a computer-based multicultural academic program.
5. Minimizing potential distractions from academic work.
6. Exploring the possibilities of long-distance education using interactive video.
7. Strengthening the involvement of parents in support of the schools.

By examining some the misunderstandings that underlie successful approaches to teaching in a multicultural environment, teachers can devise more effective methods and more challenging content for all students. Some of the more successful cooperative multicultural models view collaborative intimacy as a natural condition between teachers and students.

The collaborative process works best when teachers:

- provide students with the larger meaning (or purpose) for learning cooperative group skills.
- use active learning techniques where students can collaboratively shape alliances.
- relate what's being learned to the students personal and world environment—without compromising distinctive realities and effects.
- respect different learning styles and diverse ways of learning.
- develop collaborative learning styles, cooperation, and reciprocity.
- emphasize concrete tasks where students can assert multiple perspectives.

- communicate high expectations while respecting different ways of knowing.

A student's cultural background is a valuable tool for learning. Every student needs to learn about both academic and cultural realms to be capable of making intelligent life choices. Teaching information is one thing; teaching how to cooperatively build on a multiplicity of cultural values in a way that democratically benefits everyone is quite another. It requires a change in teaching attitudes, recognizing the merit in groups of children figuring things out for themselves. Because some students are so used to being "spoon fed," they frequently experience anguish when deciding to take action on choices. This is, at least in part, linked to the recognition of taking personal responsibility for what is happening.

Students and teachers need to become culturally curious and actively examine their own culture to extend their knowledge about the culture of others (Beane, 1990). The insights gained from the increased awareness of multiple social realities can help move the curriculum closer to the culture of each student and construct circumstances in which students of difference can thrive.

STRUCTURING A COLLABORATIVE ENVIRONMENT

Learning involves more than students and teachers. Everyone is involved, either directly in the education of children, or indirectly in structuring the world in which they live. If they can work together, politicians, business leaders, communities,parents, and teachers can revitalize our endangered educational institutions. Finding solutions to the problem of untapped human resources will require a recognition of the complex psychological, social, and institutional conditions that give rise to today's schooling difficulties (Kearns, 1987) Then we can marshal the social energy to build up the schools of the future.

Teachers have enormous power over how students view themselves. That power can be used to develop talent... or it can cause a crippling sense of inadequacy and failure. Unless the organization of the school and classroom environment provide for positive interaction between the whole spectrum of students, invalid stereotypes and preconceptions will be reinforced. If children from all races and backgrounds don't work together on an equal footing in school, then nothing is going to change the fact that they are valued differently and are not considered capable of working together for common goals.

For today's population of students academic knowledge must also connect multicultural studies with self-sufficiency and the critical thinking skills necessary for dealing with an environment where change is the one constant. Collaborative learning includes strategies for connecting thinking to cooperative group work. Students need to learn how to jointly search out information on questions generated by individuals or the group. They need to acquire and practice techniques for analyzing, interpreting, negotiating, and communicating their information as a team. And they need to learn how to be held accountable and pool their talents to help each other learn (Kraft, 1985).

The process of change is not an easy one. Outdated associations, time, and progress (as Margaret Atwood, 1988, has suggested) are not straight lines:

> *but dimensions....a shape, something you can see, like a series of liquid transparencies, one laid on top of another. You don't look back along time, but down through it, like water. Sometimes this comes to the surface, sometimes that sometimes nothing. Nothing goes away.*
> —Cat's Eye

Even as new understandings invoke new images, few educational traditions, like individual competition, seem willing to simply fade away. There are some proven models that can positively shape schooling in the future. The school reform agenda for the 1990s is beginning to include concepts like shared management, how pupils are grouped, and parental involvement. School and classroom organization are taking center stage as we approach a fundamental reordering of educational priorities.

The basic elements of cooperation and higher-level thinking skills are coming to be viewed as essential skills for today's workplace and tomorrow's workforce. The American workers of the early 21st century are *in schools today*. As far as the schools are concerned, developing a high level of interpersonal and small-group skills means going beyond ability grouping or individual assignments at the same table. Interdependence (in tasks, in terms of resources and rewards) is different from physical proximity. It also means more than having the faster students help the slower ones when their work is done. Cooperative learning places the emphasis on social solidarity and joint responsibility for reaching group goals.

When teachers emphasize competition, the result can be diminished accomplishment and alienation from school. But when a student finds out that the only way to reach his or her personal objectives is by helping everyone in the group reach *their goal* he or she is much more likely to seek outcomes beneficial to all (Johnson, Maruyama, Johnson, Nelson, & Skon, 1981). The building of a cooperative learning community can allow for collective and individual expression, even if part of the process is difficult. Encouraging higher levels of thinking, collective responsibility, and peer support for individual and team achievement are all key elements in building a cooperative learning framework.

Peer Support Structures

The more options students have open to them, the more learning takes on an element of ambiguity similar to today's world of work. Part of teaching is helping students learn how to tolerate uncertainty and consider possibilities. Students may want answers when what they need are ideas for thinking skills to grow on. Asking questions that are not fully answerable exercise the imagination and furnishes it with important intellectual values.

The peer support structures that develop as students learn to work in cooperative groups can help them deal with open-ended questions. The small group provides opportunities for trial and error, and it provides a safe environment for asking questions, expressing opinions, and taking risks. In high-spirited teams more pupils get a chance to respond, raise issues, or question ideas that are unclear. And, since each student brings unique strengths and experiences to the group, respect for individual differences can be enhanced (Meece & Blumenfeld, 1987).

Getting together in teams (to accomplish something) is a great motivator Projects and ideas are frequently pushed beyond what an individual would attempt or suggest. The quality and quantity of thinking increases as more ideas are added, surpassing what the student could do alone. Group interaction enhances idea development, and students have many opportunities to be teachers as well as learners.

Simultaneously, the small group structure extends children's resources as they are encouraged to pool strategies and share information. More withdrawn students become more active. Students who often have a hard time sticking to a task receive group assistance, so they do a better job of monitoring their time. Helping everyone become a productive group member results in group unity. This group unity has been found to extend beyond the classroom, to the playground and social situations (Ziegler, 1981).

Collaborative Teacher Development

Teachers also need to model attitudes and present themselves as problem solvers and models of inquiry. They do this by letting students know that everyone is an active learner and no one knows all the answers. By creating an environment where students are encouraged and affirmed, teachers can push the boundaries of the curriculum into new spaces.

Creating conditions under which teachers can gain and sustain knowledge themselves is just as important as creating the conditions for an enriched student-learning environment. Shared curriculum development and decision making requires knowledgeable professional (teachers) working in an environment that allows time for creative planning, research, risk taking, and thoughtful evaluation. Moving from the certainty of textbooks and teachers' manuals requires that teachers have a deep understanding of their subject matter, a thorough knowledge of the characteristics of effective instruction, and a chance to keep up to date.

Successful teacher development efforts build on the teacher's expertise and sense of professionalism. A team approach helps overcome isolation while building networks to sustain teachers. If teachers can weather this period of collective retooling, there's hope that a renaissance, rather than a dark age, is in the offing. In the final analysis, the success of any reform movement has to be based on the individual teacher's commitment, expertise, and ability to continue learning.

Social Interaction and Self-Starting Learners

The original definition of educate meant the *drawing out* of a person's talents, rather than *putting in* information. The fluid character of today's knowledge requires replacing the old model of teaching (filling the empty vessels of students' minds). In cooperative learning, teaching might be described as choreography or coaching to bring out innate abilities.

Getting students excited about a subject, and linking it personally to meaning, is an act of pedagogical leadership. When teachers take collective responsibility for how schools are managed, and students take more responsibility for their own learning, a teacher–student–learning synergy develops. Instead of rivalry, a team spirit can emerge that provides group support for internalizing ladders of knowledge and wresting personal meaning from subjects.

Educational goal structures have traditionally been teacher centered. Teachers controlled learning by imparting knowledge, maintaining control, and validating thinking. Times have changed. The skills students need for the 1990s can only be achieved by teaching learners to be self-starting thinkers who can work together to solve problems.

Small-group cooperative learning involves significant changes in the role of the classroom teacher. In the cooperative learning classroom the teacher is faced with the difficult task of encouraging students to become responsible for their own learning. One of the goals is to have students rely more heavily upon their classmates for assistance in doing a task and evaluating an answer. Only after they have checked with three or four students can they ask the teacher for help.

Teachers specify the instructional objectives, arrange the classroom to maximize social interaction, provide the appropriate materials, explain the task and the cooperative goal structure, observe the student interactions, and help students solve some of the more difficult problems. They also pay attention to the learning process, social relationships within the groups, and the evaluation or the group products.

In a collaborative setting the teacher helps children gain confidence in their own ability and the group's ability to work through problems. Gradually students come to rely as much on their peers as on the teacher. Students are motivated more by the social contact with other group members and by their sense of achievement as they succeed in challenging tasks through the group effort rather than through strict, step-by-step, teacher direction.

It is important that students understand that simply "telling an answer" or "doing someone's work" is not helping a classmate learn. There has to be some intellectual sharing. Lending assistance involves helping someone grasp the meaning or explaining with an example. These understandings need to be actively explained, demonstrated, and developed by the teacher. The role of the teacher in a new classroom setting is akin to a scientific researcher constantly testing hypotheses. They are the prime decision makers, professionals who must make thousands of educational decisions influenced by a whole range of factors.

New Responsibilities For Teachers and Students

Students in cooperative learning settings often raise questions and ideas which go beyond the teacher's guide. Teachers must also become comfortable with saying "I don't know" or "let's find out" as students push them in new learning directions that may be unimagined and unplanned. The wider the repertoire of skills, the more effective teachers become at developing strategies and capacities for selecting and combining thinking skills.

Cooperative classroom environments will not materialize overnight or without effort. Teachers need to understand and actively seek to create them. A conceptual reexamination of the organizational process and grouping structures is needed to form collaborative learning groups. When they do, many teachers will find that their best instincts about mixed-ability group work could have promoted better learning all along.

Cooperative learning has many teaching advantages. Dividing the class into groups means the teacher has five, six, or seven groups instead of 25 to 35 individuals to make good contact with each day. In addition there are 25 to 35 aides in the classroom. Pupils monitor each other while creating a spirit of cooperation and helpfulness. Students seem to become better listeners within a cooperative structure (Hertz-Lazarowitz, Sharan, & Steinberg, 1980). If the group doesn't get to the bottom of an issue, it can collectively ask for the teacher's help. This way students can formulate better questions for teacher input and use answers to develop more questions.

Cooperative learning can help teachers spend less time being policemen as students learn that they are capable of validating their own values and ideas. Teachers are freer to move about, work with small groups and interact in a more personal manner with students. Cooperative group learning can also be arranged so there is less paperwork for the teacher. Six or eight group papers is less than 24 or 32 individual ones. In this structure teachers continue to be learners, opening new channels of thinking and learning.

Attitudes Change As Students Balance Social Responsibility with Individual Freedom

Students must also undergo a major shift in values and attitudes if a collaborative learning environment is to succeed. Getting over years of learned helplessness will take time. The school experience has taught students that the teacher is there to validate their thinking and direct learning. Upon entering school, students have been constantly compared with one another for grades and recognition. For many teachers, direction on the smallest detail becomes the order of the day. Students learn that it's easy to predict their success based on their past performance. Unlearning these dated modeling structures takes time.

Attitudes change as students learn to work cooperatively (Kraft, 1985). Rather than taking individual ownership of ideas, students share recognition. They learn to evaluate the learning outcomes rather than hurrying to finish the task. Active learning teams can do all kinds of things: write collective stories, edit each others writing, solve mathematics problems, correct homework, prepare for tests, investigate science questions, examine artifacts, work on a computer simulation, brainstorm an invention, create a sculpture, or arrange a new rap music tune.

Working together students can synthesize what they have learned by giving a presentation, coauthoring a written summary, or communicating a concept through the subtleties of the arts. Within cooperative learning groups a student's role as collaborative researcher replaces the traditional notion of student as a passive knowledge recipient. Learning starts with curiosity, moves toward students' interpretation of the subject's meaning in their lives, and is then connected to other areas of knowledge. Children learn by "talking out," assimilating ideas through group interaction, and assuming a high level of responsibility for what they set out to learn. Collaboration becomes more a "culture" or set of values (that pervades the classroom) than a technique.

New models for teaching and learning require new school and classroom structures. The need for new learning strategies and organizational patterns is interwoven with political, social, and economic support. Without a societal commitment—and sustained effort—it is difficult to talk about empowering teachers or improving the texture and richness of learning.

The public and leaders in every field are coming to agree that starving our educational institutions can destroy our civic culture and prevent the private sector retooling necessary for serving the needs of the 1990s and beyond. This means that school policies, structures, and curriculum are being pushed to keep up with a new world where people must live and work effectively in relationship with others. Within the cooperative learning classroom, civic responsibility and personal freedom come from exercising choices in meaningful group activities. They develop as a result of collaborative experiences, as students struggle with problems and learn not only to solve them, but learn that they *can* solve them.

Balancing responsibility and freedom involves a rejection of the insufficient, an imaging of a better state or collective thing...a fight and a leap ahead in thinking, at once a refusal and a realization.
—Sartre

REFERENCES

Abraham, S.Y., & Campbell, C. (1984). *Peer teachers as mirrors and monitors*. Detroit, MI: Wayne State University.

Ammon, P., & Ammon, M.S. (1987). Hidden resources in the reading and writing of bilingual children. In M.P. Douglas (Ed.), *Claremont Reading Conference 51st Yearbook*. Claremont, CA: Claremont University Press.

Atwood, M. (1988). *Cat's eye*. New York: Doubleday.

Baida, P. (1990). *Poor Richard's legacy: American business values from Benjamin Franklin to Donald Trump*. New York: William Morrow.

Beane, J.A. (1990). *Affect in the curriculum: Toward democracy, dignity, and diversity*. New York: Teachers College Press.

Brophy, J., & Good, T. (1986). Teacher behavior and student achievement. In M.C. Wittrock (Ed.), *Research on teaching*. New York: St. Martin's Press.

Carnegie Foundation for the Advancement of Teaching. (1986). Task Forum on education and the economy. *A nation prepared: Teachers for the 21st century*. New York: Author.

Cohen, E. (1986). *Designing group work*. New York: Teachers College Press.

DeVries, D., & Slavin, R. (1978). Teams-games-tournaments (TGT): Review of ten classroom experiments. *Journal of Research and Development in Education, 12*, 28-38.

Education Commission of the States. (1988). *One third of a nation: A report of the commission on minority participation in education and American life*. Washington, DC: American Council on Education.

Educational Researcher Editors. (1985). Cooperative learning: A research success story. *Educational Researcher, 3*.

Hertz-Lazarowitz, R., Sharan, S., & Steinberg, R. (1980). Classroom learning styles of elementary school children. *Journal of Educational Psychology, 72*, 99-106.

Jager Adams, M. (1990). *(1990). Beginning to read: Thinking and learning about print*. Cambridge, MA: MIT Press.

Johnson, D., & Johnson, R. (1974). *Learning together and alone: Cooperation, competition, and individualization.* Englewood Cliffs, NJ: Prentice-Hall.

Johnson, D.W., & Johnson, R. (1989). *Cooperation and competition: Theory and research.* Edna, MN: Interaction Book Co.

Johnson, D.W., Maruyama, G., Johnson, R., Nelson, D., & Skon, L. (1981). Effects of cooperative competitive, and individualistic goal structures on achievement: A meta analysis. *Psychological Bulletin, 89,* 47-62.

Kearns, D. (1987). *Winning the brain race: A bold plan to make our schools competitive.* San Francisco: Institute for Contemporary Studies Press.

Kraft, R.G. (1985). Group inquiry turns passive students active. *College Teaching, 33*(4), 149-54.

Levine, M., & Trachtman, R. (Eds.). (1988). *American business and the public education.* New York: Teachers College Press.

Meece, J.L., & Blumenfeld, P.C. (1987, April). *Elementary school children's motivational orientation and patterns of engagement in classroom activities.* Paper presented at American Educational Research Association, Washington, DC.

Newmann, F. M., & Thompson, J. (1987). *Effects of cooperative learning on achievement in secondary schools: A summary of research.* Madison, WI: University of Wisconsin, National Center on Effective Secondary Schools.

Phillips, K. (1990). *The politics of rich and poor: Wealth and the American electorate in the Reagan aftermath.* New York: Random House.

Sarte, J.P. (1963). *Search for a method.* New York: Alfred A. Knopf.

Schorr, L., & Schorr, D. (1989). *Within our reach: Breaking the cycle of disadvantage.* New York: Anchor Press.

Sharan, S. (1980). Cooperative learning in small groups: Recent methods and effects on achievement, attitudes and ethnic relations. *Review of Educational Research, 50,* 241-271.

Sharan, S., & Shachar, H. (1988). *Language and learning in the cooperative classroom.* New York: Springer-Verlag.

Shea Bayer, A. (1990). *Collaborative apprenticeship learning.* Mountainview, CA: Mayfield Publishing.

Slavin, R. (1983). *Cooperative learning.* New York: Longman.

Slavin, R. (1987). *Cooperative learning: Student teams.* Washington, DC: National Education Association.

Slavin, R. (1988). Cooperative learning and student achievement. *Educational Leadership, 54,* 31-33.

Slavin R. (1989). *School and classroom organization.* Hillsdale, NJ: Erlbaum.

Slavin, R.E. (1986). *Using student team learning* (3rd ed.). Baltimore, MD: Center for Research on Elementary and Middle Schools, John Hopkins University.

Slavin, R., Sharan, S., Kagan, S., Hertz-Lazarowitz, R., Webb, C., & Schmuck, R. (Eds). (1985). *Learning to cooperate, cooperating to learn.* New York: Plenum Publishing.

Webb, N.M. (1982). Student interaction and learning in small groups. *Review of Educational Research, 52,* 421-445.

Ziegler, S. (1981). The effectiveness of cooperative learning teams for increasing cross-ethnic friendship. *Human Organization, 40,* 264-268.

2

DIFFERENT APPROACHES TO COOPERATIVE LEARNING

Cooperative learning has been researched for more than 20 years, and its effectiveness was established long before the current concern about tracking became widespread. It was originally developed to respond to student motivation...which is improved by having students work together to master what the teacher has taught
—Robert Slavin

Cooperative learning, as an approach to classroom organization, is beginning to show up in school improvement recommendations and teachers' lesson plans. It's also an important topic for debate in educational journals and school staff rooms. One thing is certain: The individual teacher in the classroom is the critical factor in changing instructional procedures for the better.

Cooperative group interaction can start by having students help each other in solving problems and completing academic tasks. The next step is to combine this idea with positive interdependence between group members and individual accountability. Like any instructional strategy, implementing cooperative learning principles requires multiple objectives and approaches. Teachers also need to experience various methods of cooperative learning to really understand the power of the technique (Moore Johnson, 1990).

No combination of cooperative learning strategies is best for everyone all the time. However, it is fair to suggest that there is solid evidence for including cooperative groups as part of any teacher's professional repertoire. We now have plenty of reliable data supporting the notion that students can profit both socially and academically from working with peers in collaborative settings (Sharan, 1980).

Cooperative, Competitive, and Individualized Learning Methods

The most common classroom structures in use today are individualized learning, competitive learning, and increasingly, *cooperative learning,* (Good & Brophy, 1989).

Individualized Learning. In individualized learning structures, each student works at his or her own pace and expects to be left alone by other students. The individual takes a major part of the responsibility for completing the task, evaluating his or her progress toward task completion and the quality of his or her effort. The goal or task objective is perceived as important for each student, and each student expects to achieve the goal. Types of instructional activities center around specific skill and knowledge acquisition. The assignment is clearly defined, and behavior is specified to avoid confusion and the need for extra help. The teacher is the major source for assistance, support, and reinforcement.

Competitive Learning. When competitive goal structures exist, the goal is not perceived to be of large importance to the students, and they can accept either winning or losing. Each student expects to have an equal change to enjoy the activity (win or lose). Students monitor the progress of their competitors and compare ability, skills, and knowledge with peers. Instructional activities tend to focus on skill practice, knowledge recall, and review. The assignments are clear, with rules for competing specified. The teacher is the major resource and often directs the competitive activity.

Cooperative Learning. The goal of a cooperative learning team must be seen as important for each student, and group members should expect to achieve the group objectives. It helps if each student expects positive interaction where students share ideas and materials. In cooperative groups each member is responsible for a particular task and accountable for his or her own knowledge or area of contribution to the group. All group members are expected to contribute to the group effort. Dividing the tasks among them capitalizes on the diversity of learning styles. Students receive support for risk taking, and all are expected to make contributions to the group effort. Other group members (students) are perceived to be the major source for assistance, support, and reinforcement. When the learning team is interdependent, students know that they play a unique role and that the team loses if they don't put out individual effort (Haines & McKeachie, 1967).

The Process of Cooperative Learning

Cooperative learning includes a number of techniques involving learners in group work. Teachers can pick and choose various elements of the process after becoming acquainted with the major approaches and understanding how to use key elements to achieve differing results. To be most successful, teachers need careful preparation and skillful application. Like any other new teaching concept, cooperative learning takes training, practice and repetition over time (Carkhuff, 1985).

For individuals new to group learning, direct training (where groups actually immerse themselves in the cooperative learning process) is recommended. The actual hands-on, minds-on interaction with the peers raises awareness and instills confidence in a way that reading or hearing about this strategy cannot. After training and some initial experiences in the classroom the rough edges can be smoothed through additional reading, practice, and on-site peer mentoring. In addition, teacher workshops and university classes can help—especially when teachers try activities, share experiences, and give and receive feedback within a collegial structure that supports collaboration.

It is often helpful for teachers to start with cooperative learning by working in learning teams with colleagues—planning, gathering materials, and carrying out combined activities involving more than one classroom. At this stage teachers need coaching, not evaluation. Just the fact that they are trying to use collaborative structures is a good sign that teachers are growing professionally by keeping up with current research and tested practice.

MAJOR APPROACHES TO COOPERATIVE LEARNING

Student Teams and Achievement Divisions (STAD) (R. Slavin)

The Student Teams Achievement Divisions has five components:

1. *Class presentation*
   Each week a new material is first presented by the teacher to the whole class in a lecture, discussion, or video technology format.
2. *Teams.*
   Students are assigned to four- or five-member learning teams. Each team represents a cross section of the class, made up of high-, average-, and low-achieving students, girls and boys, students of differing ethnic, racial, and economic backgrounds.
   Team members work together to study worksheets the teacher has

made, which consist of problems and information to be mastered. They may work in pairs, discuss problems as a group, quiz each other, or use whatever strategy they like to master the material. Teams are also given answer sheets. Group members and reminded that their task is to learn the concept, not just come up with the correct answer to the problems. Students are instructed to keep studying until they are sure everyone understands the material.

3. *Quizzes*

    After the team practices, each student takes a quiz on the material they have been studying. The quizzes assess individual achievement on the material presented and practiced in class. Group members may not help individuals on the quizzes.

4. *Individual Improvement Scores*

    A scoring system allows students to earn points for their team based on individual improvement over past performance.

5. *Team Recognition*

    Teams are recognized for high individual performance and high team scores. Social recognition such as weekly class newsletters, bulletin board displays, or weekly class radio announcements are used as rewards for individuals and teams (Slavin, 1987).

STAD can be used with materials especially designed for Student Team Learning and available from John Hopkins Team Learning Project, or it can be used with teacher-made materials. It's easy for teachers to make their own materials. The materials needed include a worksheet an answer sheet, and a quiz for each unit planned. Units should take 3 to 5 days of instruction. STAD instruction involves dividing students into teams, teaching the lesson, arranging for team study time, testing, recording, and recognizing teams and individuals.

In the STAD approach teachers assign learning teams rather than letting students choose teams themselves. Each team is composed of students whose performance levels range from low to high. The average performance level of all the teams should be about equal. This is done so that students can tutor each other and so that no single team will have an academic performance advantage. Many teachers achieve this by rank-ordering students on past performance, test scores, or teacher judgment.

Each lesson in STAD begins with a presentation. A good lesson focuses on meaning, involves students in active learning, uses good demonstrations, asks higher order thinking questions, and moves along at a good pace. Objectives should be clearly spelled out so that students know what they are expected to learn.

During team student and problem solving the team member's job is to learn the material presented in the lesson and help his or her teammates. Each team receives only a few worksheets to enable students to work together. Members are encouraged to explain answers to each other rather than simply write down the correct response. It is important to grade quizzes quickly and recognize team accomplishments (Slavin, 1989).

Teams–Games–Tournaments (TGT) (D. DeVries & R. Slavin)

The teams–games–tournaments is the same as STAD except it replaces quizzes with a game or tournament. Students compete as representative of their team with others who are judged like them in academic standing.

Games are played at tables of three or four students, each of whom represents a separate team. Tournaments frequently consist of questions or challenge problems printed out for students. Questions are simple, relevant to the content, and designed to challenge the targeted group. Games can be constructed by numbered questions on a quiz sheet or oral questions given by the teacher.

Learning Together (LT) (Johnson & Johnson)

Students work together on a group project or assignment sheet. Each group hands in a single group product or assignment sheet. They are rewarded with praise, grades, or tokens based on group performance and how well they work together rather than on individual scores.

Jigsaw (JIG) (E. Aronson)

Each student in the group is given separate bits of information to student on a topic, such as different aspects of a country or different short stories on a topic, such as different aspects of a country or different short stories by an author. In their groups they share what they have discovered. They then go to "expert" groups where they further broaden their knowledge before returning to their original team to tutor their teammates. Students are tested individually over all the material and receive individual scores. Positive effects on both achievement and cross-ethnic friendship have been found using this approach.

Jigsaw II (JIG II) (Modified from JIG by R. Slavin)

All students are given the same material to study. Students become experts and then teach the group specific subtopics such as the early life of Abraham Lincoln, his early political life, his presidency, his political ideals, and his untimely death. Team scores are calculated from individual quiz scores and are publicized in a class newsletter.

Group Investigation (GI) (S. Sharan and colleagues)

Each group is assigned a different project. Students research the topic of their group, organize material, and present findings to the class. Each team decides the best way to do this. The emphasis is on higher-level learning, applying and synthesizing ideas, and drawing inferences.

Team-Accelerated Instruction (TAI) (R. Slavin)

This mathematics technique was developed for elementary students with too diverse an ability range to be taught the same material at the same rate. Each student gets a diagnostic test. Each then works through a sequence of units at her own pace, but teammates work in pairs, checking each other's work and tests. Team scores are based on individual scores and on work covered. Certificates are awarded to the team.

Cooperative Integrated Reading and Composition (CIRC)

This technique for reading and writing in upper elementary grades pairs students to work on engaging activities such as summarizing stories and mastering comprehension. Students are assigned to teams and work in mixed-ability partnerships. While the teacher is working with one group, students in the other groups read to one another, make predictions about the story, respond to questions, or practice writing skills. During language arts class students are involved in writing drafts, revising, and editing each other's work for oral presentation or publication. CIRC activities follow a learning sequence: teacher instruction, team practice, preassessments, and a quiz. Teammates decide when each student is ready for a quiz. Team rewards are certificates based on the average performance of group members. Because all students work at a level appropriate to their ability, students have equal opportunities for success.

Variations and Differences

The first six popular approaches mentioned here are general and can be used across grades and subject areas. Programs can vary in terms of both task structures, role assignment, team scores, and what counts toward reward contingencies.

Some approaches give group rewards based on the individual team member's achievement. Others may not give group rewards or choose to reward the group as a whole with no individual achievement basis. The patterns of tasks and reward structures can be divided into four parts:

1. Group rewards based on individual achievement. (STAD, TGT, TAI, and CIRC)
2. Group rewards not based on individual achievement or no group reward. All students doing the same task. (LT)
3. Group rewards based on individual achievement with all students working on different tasks. (JIG II)
4. Group rewards not based on individual achievement or no group reward with students doing different tasks. (JIG GI)

The ways chosen to manage rewards, tasks, and accountability will do more to influence potential outcomes than any other factor (Hertz-Lazarowitz, Sharan, & Steinberg, 1980).

Accountability

Accountability ensures that both teachers and students are contributing to a common goal. Individual accountability gives teachers a way of checking what part each student is playing in the group's work (Eagen, 1986). Individual accountability is accomplished through:

1. Group rewards that are based on individual quizzes
2. Having students make individual presentations on a group project or do unique tasks in their group which contribute to an overall goal. For example, one group member reports on the homes of the Navaho Indians, one reports on foods, another on rituals, etc.
3. Providing incentive for students to work together to learn new material, but being tested individually.

Group accountability is also essential. If students are discussing last night's basketball game instead of working on mathematics, they aren't going to benefit from group learning. Teachers must clearly define the task and closely monitor groups to ensure they are on task (Sansone, 1986).

Shared Responsibility and Group Roles

Collaborative groups structures involve shared responsibilities. This means that a variety of tasks must be performed by group members. Each member of a group assumes the charge of making sure that group members work toward a group goal or objective. When students are new to cooperative learning and during some initial experiences, teachers may wish to assign certain roles to group participants. Some of the most frequent group tasks include:

1. Facilitator
   - organizes the group's work
   - makes certain students understand the group's job
   - takes the group's questions and concerns to the teacher *after* the group attempts a solution and tries alternatives.
2. Checker
   - checks with group members to make sure that everyone understands their task
   - checks to be sure that everyone agrees with the group response and can explain it.
3. Reader
   - reads the problem or directions to the group
4. Recorder
   - writes the groups response or data collection on a group response sheet or log.
5. Encourager
   - offers support and encouragement to group members. Keeps others feeling good about working together (Johnson & Johnson, 1974).

All students assume responsibility for promoting and maintaining positive attitudes and a positive group spirit. This doesn't mean using the "team spirit" to suppress dissent or intimidate individuals.

All of these responsibilities involve specific skills and behaviors:

1. Clarifying and elaborating—interpreting information or building on information from another group member.
2. *Providing information or giving opinions*—sharing relevant knowledge and ideas with the group.
3. *Seeking facts, data, or opinions from group members*—searching out and requesting relevant information
4. *Summarizing*—recapitulating and pulling together the group's shared knowledge and information.
5. *Guiding and Managing*—establishing a process which helps the group achieve its goal or learning objective.

Organizing a group plan of action is an important part of shared leadership. Learning how to search out, share, and receive information to continue progress on a group task are important skills in working collaboratively. Students also need to learn how to summarize and clarify that information so as to move the group in the direction of completing their task or goal. Sometimes it may be necessary to test the consensus of a group—how many members agree that a particular direction is advisable or that a particular conclusion is accurate. Other task behaviors include:

- getting the group started
- staying on task
- getting the group back to work
- taking turns
- asking questions
- following directions
- staying in the group space
- keeping tack of time
- helping without giving the answer (Kraft, 1985).

Group Support Systems

In addition to helping the group reach its goal and get the job done, a group members also has the responsibility to show support and empathy for other group members and their feelings. It is important to reflect on the group process and the feelings group members express. This assures that individual group members have opportunities to express ideas and opinions. When group interactions become tense, a release of that tension is needed; perhaps a funny joke will ease members' frustrations. Harmony can often be achieved when a group member acknowledges that another group member is upset.

Support or maintenance behaviors include the skills of:

1. *Compromising*—coming to an agreement by meeting half way, "giving in" to other group members when necessary
2. *Empathizing and encouraging*—showing understanding and helping others feel a part of the group
3. *Gatekeeping*—creating harmony in the group
5. *Expressing group feelings*—helping the group to examine how it is feeling and operating

Other support or maintenance behaviors include:

- using names
- encouraging others to talk
- responding to ideas
- using eye contact
- showing appreciation

- disagreeing in a pleasant way
- criticizing an idea, not a person
- keeping things under control
- paraphrasing

It is helpful for groups to evaluate the effectiveness of each group meeting as soon as it is over. This provides feedback and insights into the collaborative process. As the group members learn to focus energy on the learning task, they also learn to identify with the group process—helping members grow and develop. Compromising, creating harmony, sharing, and encouraging are learned behaviors. They take time, coaching, and commitment. When group responsibility and support behaviors are in balance, group members can work collaboratively to achieve important group objectives (Jussim, 1986).

Group Evaluation and Processing: Possible Questions

1. How did your group get started on its task?
2. Did your group do something different from other groups?
3. Did your group approach the problem or task effectively?
4. How did your group reach agreement on your answer?
5. Are you satisfied with the way your group recorded the information? Would you do it differently next time?
6. How did working in a group help you?
7. What helped your group stick to its task?
8. How did you feel working in this group?
9. How did you offer support to other members of the group?
10. How did your group share information and ideas?
11. Which social skill will your group use more of next time?
12. Did your group accomplish its tasks? What did you learn?

Solving Problems and Resolving Conflict

The ability to solve problems and smoothly resolve conflict in the group are important asks of cooperation and collaboration. When conflict arises, group members often take unyielding stances and refuse to consider other points of view. Group members need strategies for negotiating and problem solving to successfully defuse conflict and create harmony (New Society Publishers, 1989). Some conflict strategies include:

1. *Withdrawal*—the individual withdraws from interaction, recognizing that the goal and the interaction are not important enough to be in conflict over.

2. *Forcing*—the task is more important than the relationship; members use all their energy to get the task done.
3. *Smoothing*—the relationship is more than the task; individuals want to be liked and accepted.
4. *Compromising*—the task and the relationship are both important, but both members must agree to gain something and lose something.
5. *Confrontation*—Task and relationship are equally important, the conflict is defined as a problem-solving situation (Filley, 1975).

Problem solving is a useful group strategy to assist in conflict resolution. This systematic five-step process of constructively addressing conflicts involves:

1. Defining the problem and its causes.
2. Generating alternative solutions to the problem.
3. Examining advantages and disadvantages to each alternative.
4. Deciding upon and implementing the most desirable solution.
5. Evaluating whether the solutions solve the problem.

Group members must define exactly what the problem is. On occasion, this can be difficult, but it is worth the effort. Once the problem is defined, group members can then suggest alternative solutions for the problem and explore the consequences of each of those alternatives. The group members then make a decision to try an alternative and to review the results within a stipulated period of time (Spivack, Platt, & Shure, 1976).

It can also be important to teach *confrontation skills* and techniques for *successful resolution*. Some of these suggestions include teaching students to:

1. Describe behavior; do not evaluate, label, accuse, or insult.
2. Define the conflict as a mutual problem, not a win–lose situation.
3. Use "I" statements.
4. Communicate what you think and feel.
5. Be critical of ideas, not people; affirm other's competence.
6. Give everyone a chance to be heard.
7. Follow the guidelines for rational argument.
8. Make sure there is enough time for discussion
9. Take the other person's perspective (Stanford, 1976).

Negotiating is also a learning part of problem resolution. It involves mutual discussion and arrangement of the terms of an agreement. The process of learning to "read" another's behavior for clues to a problem solution is crucial in being able to guess what will appeal to another person and how to make a deal in which each participant's preferences or needs are considered.

Complementing the task and support behaviors are such communication skills as active listening. This means both attending and responding to group and individual efforts. Active listening allows all group members to be fully in tune with each other. Acknowledging the content, feelings, or meaning of what another person is communicating lends itself to goodwill and understanding. Gatekeeping (giving everyone a chance to express his or her ideas) assures that all members of the group participate and are secure in the knowledge that they are contributing to the group.

Organizing the Collaborative Classroom

Cooperative learning will not take place with students sitting in rows facing the teacher. Desks must be pushed together in small groups (two or more) or replaced with small tables to facilitate group interaction. Resource and hands-on materials must be made readily accessible. Collaboration will not occur in a classroom which requires students to raise their hands to talk or move out of their desks. Responsible behavior needs to be developed and encouraged. Authoritarian approaches to discipline will not work if students are expected to be responsible for their own learning and behavior (Stallings & Stipels, 1986).

Other changes involve the noise level in the room. Sharing and working together, even in controlled environments, will be louder than in an environment where students work silently from textbooks. Teachers need to tolerate higher noise levels and learn to evaluate whether or not they're constructive.

Evaluating cooperative learning requires a variety of procedures. In spite of new evaluative techniques on the horizon, some learning outcomes will probably continue to be measured by such instruments as standardized tests, quizzes, and written exams. Fortunately, new tests that have open-ended questions and problem-solving functions are starting to be used. Cooperative learning demands additional subjective measures like portfolios and holistic grading. Students and teachers need to be involved in evaluating learning products, the classroom climate, and individual skill development. Informal observation can view progress on things like self-esteem, discipline, cooperative, values, expression, and individual and group achievement. This process should involve self-evaluation, peer evaluation and teacher assessment.

Interactive organizational models can help teachers apply cooperative curriculum constructs in their classrooms. As they organize interactive learning environments, children learn to shape questions, interpret data, and make connections between subjects. When small learning groups are formed, under teacher direction, students can learn to take responsibility for their own learning and assist others. This means collaboration instead of competition.

When task-oriented work groups combine student initiative with social responsibility, students with less information can stimulate the students with more—and vice versa. The same thing is true when it comes to teaching thinking processes like comprehension, decision making, and problem solving.

Various heterogeneous group structures can help students set personal learning agendas (Sharan & Shachar, 1988). They can also provide the structure for the joint application to critical thinking skills—distinguishing hypotheses from verified information and recognizing reasoning based on misconceptions (Kuhn, Amsel, & O'Loughlin, 1988). Cooperative groups invite students to be active players in classroom activities. Topical projects, writing assignments, problem solving, and journal reaction papers are examples of activities that require group planning, negotiating, and the collaborative distribution of work.

As groups to try to reach consensus, they can create an analysis grid whereby comparisons and contrasts can be made as well as students' speculations about outcomes. Within the tension of discussing different points of view (even heated discussion), learning takes place. Group activities can be brought to closure by forming a panel or roundtable. Students can also be assigned the cooperative task of meeting with another group to explain the conclusions reached in their work group.

Establishing the classroom conditions for the successful use of cooperative learning means more than having educators decide that it is an appropriate organizational method for enhancing learning. Students must also develop collaborative skills for mixed ability pairs or groups to work productively. The basic elements of this positive group work involves face-to-face interaction, social skills, individual accountability, and group processing (Sharan, 1980).

Changes In the Learning Environment

Researchers who are concerned with the inequality of learning possibilities fostered by traditional classroom organization suggest that we should reduce the general preoccupation with competition and ability grouping. Cooperative learning would also appear to have a natural role to play in overcoming the suppression of human aspirations that have played such a negative role in competitive tracking models (Ziegler, 1981).

Changing classroom organizational patterns and teaching strategies requires systematic staff development and the association of like-minded colleagues. It also takes time, practice, and systematic support for the vital energy inherent in new skills to become part of teachers' repertoires. Changes in the organization of learning requires an environment where it is safe to make mistakes and where it is safe to learn from those mistakes. Cooperative learning is only as good as the ability to its practitioners to model the behavior. For the teacher the best way to deal with team spirit in the classroom is to model the behavior and join in.

Aids To Collaborative Learning

The approaches described here are all fairly easy to use. However, the change in classroom structure is dramatic. Students begin helping each other learn rather resenting those who know the answers or making fun of those who do not. The teacher is viewed more as a resource. Learning is seen as social, fun, and under their control. In a spirit of camaraderie learners create a climate of acceptance.

The research suggests that:

- Collaboration works best when students are given real problems to solve.
- A collaborative environment grows slowly, nurtured by teachers who consider everyone a resource.
- Learning to think as a team that "sinks or swims" together can help many students learn more.
- A collaborative environment works best if it allows risks and mistakes.
- Collaborative learning allows practice in solving problems.
- Individual learn best when they are held individually responsible for group subtasks.
- The less academically talented develop better learning attitudes when they work directly with "successful students.
- Roles of ten change; student as tutor or teacher—and teacher as learner (Hord, Rutherford, Huling-Austin, & Hall, 1987).

Suggestions for Small Group Collaboration

It often takes several attempts with cooperative learning techniques to get groups working effectively. Like teachers, students must be gradually eased into the process through a consistent routine. The more teachers and students work in groups, the easier it becomes. Some students may encounter initial problems, because they are accustomed to being rewarded for easy-to-come-by answers that require little thinking. It may take some time and teacher assistance for them to become comfortable working cooperatively with more ambiguity (Webb, 1982).

Some useful strategies for helping students adjust include:

- Adjust the group size to suit the activity. Groups of three or four work well for many activities like mathematics problem solving. Groups of five to seven work better for activities that require larger group participation or are more complicated (creative dramatics, larger social studies projects, certain writing projects, etc.).

- Accept a higher working noise level in the classroom.
- Do not interrupt a group that is working well. If a group seems to be floundering, ask a student to describe what the group is discussing or what part of the problem is causing difficulty. Try not to speak loudly to a group across the room. Go to them if you want to say something.
- Experiement with different group patterns and size.
- Try interacting with the groups from time to time. *Listen* to their discussions
  - Individuals must check with other members of the group before they may raise their hands to ask the teacher for help. Help can then be given to the group collectively.
  - Try to reach a group consensus on a problem.
  - All students should participate.
  - Be considerate of others.
  - Students are to help any group member who asks.
- Promote involvement by all students
  - Select a group leader to be responsible for the group's work
  - Identify a recorder to write group's responses
  - Encourage students who do not appear to be actively participating

Since many teachers have little experience with cooperative learning it is taking time for this research proven technique to work its way into widespread daily practice. Implementation will take time, patience, and teaching skill. It's a challenge, but not an insurmountable one.

REFERENCES

Carkhuff, R. (1985). *The art of helping: Trainer's guide*. Amherst, MA: Human Resource Development Press.

Eagen G. (1986). *The skilled helper: A Systematic approach to effective helping*. Belmont, CA: Wadsworth.

Filley, A.C. (1975). *Interpersonal conflict resolution*. Glenview, IL.: Scott Foresman.

Good, T.L., & Brophy, J. (1989). Teaching the lesson. In R. Slavin (Ed.), *School and classroom organization*. Hillsdale, NJ: Erlbaum.

Haines, D. B., & McKewachie, W. J. (1967). Cooperation verses competitive discussion methods. *Journal of Educational Psychology, 58,* 386-390.

Hertz-Lazarowitz, R., Sharan, S., & Steinberg, R. (1980). Classroom learning styles of elementary school children. *Journal of Educational Psychology, 72,* 99-106.

Hord, S., Rutherford, W., Huling-Austin, L., & Hall, G. (1987). *Taking charge of change*. Alexandria, VA: Association for Supervision and Curriculum Development.

Johnson, D.W., & Johnson, R.T. (1974). *Learning together and alone: Cooperation, competition, and individualization*. Englewood Cliffs, NJ: Prentice-Hall.

Jussim, L. (1986). Self-fulfilling prophecies: A theoretical and integrative review. *Psychological Review, 93,* 429–445.

Kraft, R. G. (1985). Group inquiry turns passive students active. *College Teaching, 33*(4), 149–154.

Kuhn, D., Amsel, E., & O'Loughlin, M. (1988). *The development of scientific thinking skills.* San Diego, CA: Academic Press.

Moore Johnson, S. (1990). *Teachers at work: Achieving success in our schools.* New York: Basic Books.

New Society Publishers. (1989). *The friendly classroom for a small planet: Collected activities, workshop plans, and songs that teach skill in cooperation and conflict resolution.* Santa Cruz, CA: New Society Publishers.

Sansone, C. (1986). A question of competence: The effects of competence and task feedback on intrinsic interest. *Journal of Personality and Social Psychology, 51,* 232–257.

Sharan, S. (1980). Cooperative learning in small groups: Recent methods and effects on achievement, attitudes and ethnic relations. *Review of Educational Research, 50,* 241–271.

Sharan, S., & Shachar, H. (1988). *Language and learning in the cooperative classroom.* New York: Springer-Verlag.

Slavin, R. (1987). *Cooperative learning: Student teams.* Washington, DC: National Education Association.

Slavin, R.E. (1989). *School and classroom organization.* Hillsdale, NJ: Erlbaum.

Spivack, G., Platt, J., & Shure, M. (1976). *The problem solving approach to adjustment.* San Francisco: Jossey Bass.

Stallings, J., & Stipek, D. (1986). Research on early childhood and elementary school teaching programs. In M. Wittrock (Ed.), *Handbook of research on teaching and learning.* New York: Macmillan.

Stanford, B. (Ed.). (1976). *Peacemaking: A guide to conflict resolution for individuals, groups, and nation.* New York: Bantam.

Webb, N.M. (1982). Student interaction and learning in small groups. *Review of Educational Research, 52,* 421–445.

Ziegler, S. (1981). The effectiveness of cooperative learning teams for increasing cross-ethnic friendship. Additional evidence. *Human Organization, 40,* 264–268.

3

LITERACY AND COOPERATIVE LEARNING

Connecting Writing, Reading, Thinking, and Learning

Sticks and stones can break your bones...but words can do permanent damage.
—Eric Bogosian

Interest in cooperative learning has grown at the very time some of the routinized and competitive notions about teaching language arts and reading are changing. In a classroom environment where collaboration and thinking are emphasized, the teacher can set the problem and organize students into small groups so that they can collaborate in working it out. This kind of active multiability group work and peer tutoring has proved to be a useful vehicle for gaining social insights, enhancing creativity, and learning basic literacy skills (Bruffee, 1984). The key to making cooperative groups work is to have students perceive that they can reach their learning goals only if other groups members reach their goals as well.

Programs to incorporate interpersonal skills into the language arts curriculum are being initiated throughout the country. The purpose is to develop practical collaborative tools through which children can use communication tools to articulate what they are thinking and feeling. Cooperative learning can also help shift control to students during reading and writing lessons.

The social process of literacy grows best when small groups work together to discuss and reflect on what they are writing and reading (Vygotsky, 1986). Social interaction can help individuals extract meaning from text, especially when small groups share together in a caring manner (Linfors, 1987). This involves children helping one another construct meaning with tools from the language arts. These response groups can play an extremely important role in literature-based curriculum.

Having students work together in small discussion groups can help them accomplish shared objectives and connect what they are learning to their environment (Flood & Lapp, 1989). Fostering dialogue and mutual consensus about difficulties in the world outside school is important, since real-world problems tend to be less well structured than those found in the curriculum. Additionally, the group process and creative thinking skills brought to bear on such problems will better prepare students for adulthood (Short, 1988).

Structuring Collaborative Whole Language Learning

Writers in the world outside of school often collaborate to help the act of writing, insight, and feeling come together more powerfully. To further students' understanding this point, teachers can encourage them to randomly examine a library shelf, magazine, or scholarly journal to spot how many works are jointly authored. In group discussions of coauthored stories—or writing together—students must know when to assume different roles, like researcher, summarizer, animator (activator), or recorder.

Pairing students is the easiest way to introduce them to the mixed-ability group experience. They can be randomly assigned, pupils can choose, or students can write down four people they would like to work with and the teacher chooses from the list. Larger groups can be formed from these two persons teams to analyze, synthesize, and evaluate language activities.

When learning tasks are assigned, it is helpful if the students know what aspects of the work are for individuals, pairs, and small groups. It is also up to the teacher to point out the goals of a lesson, placing students in groups and making sure that the right materials are available. The teacher encourages group work, monitors progress, and assesses student performance.

Some teachers like to assign different group roles so that students can experience and develop the strategies for dealing with isolated, overly talkative, or non-task-oriented group members. This allows them to practice strategies of good listening, clarifying, or disagreeing in a non-threatening manner. Groups can even be stopped from time to time while a randomly selected student summarizes what has been said—or individuals write down what they have heard. Perceptions can then be compared (Hansen, 1987).

In the last few years teachers have been trying to move from basal readers to reading real books—literature. This whole language approach has proven to have a positive effect on reading ability—as well as a profound effect on children's writing. If children read good writing, it has a positive effect on their own writing (Burns, Roe, & Ross, 1988). In a student-centered language arts/reading curriculum, children can use peer teaching techniques in active group activities that build on positive interdependence.

In "whole language" literacy circles, students are helped by the process of communicating with peer writers (real readers) who provide immediate feedback during the writing or revision process. Children need to develop the skill to go beyond stating "the introduction is good" to asking "how did your story fulfill the expectations your introduction set up?" Such student-centered higher-level group question are also an essential part of the cooperative group writing process (Solomon & Claire, 1984). Having children share a brief passage with their group can also heighten interest in what other group members may want to read in the future.

In collaborative frameworks for literacy instruction students are encouraged to discuss the work they are doing on writing projects, problems they are solving, or books they are reading. Teachers can vary the way this is done. At times, the issues they read or write about can be a topic for group discussion; at other times, students can help structure the framework for discussion, evaluating evidence, making predictions, or developing a line of thought.

By moving activities built on collaboration and higher order thinking skills into the center of the curriculum, students can assimilate concepts through peer interaction (Resnick, 1987). The national report *Becoming a Nation of Readers* points out that children spend less than 7% of their time in the classroom actually reading. Paradoxically, the research suggests that the more time they spend reading, the better they do on reading achievement tests (Conley, 1987). There is no question that actually reading books—or having the teacher read aloud—has a positive effect on the reading process.

The current research and theory in the learning and teaching of the language arts supports the use of literature for the development of student literacy (Nagy, 1988). Further, research and theory favor the use of whole, meaningful works rather than excepts or revisions (Conley, 1987). Nevertheless, many reading programs in elementary schools still depend on basal reading systems that focus on discrete skills and the use of contrived stories that have a controlled vocabulary.

Educators are currently struggling to bring practice in literacy instruction into harmony with current knowledge by shifting from basal reading system to literature-based approaches. Some school districts devote 2 or 3 days a week to the basal reading series, the rest to whole language teaching with a literature base. Others adapt some of the activities in the teacher's edition for children's literature: reading logs, time lines, maps, flow charts, and Venn diagrams.

Whatever the arrangement, whole language instruction provides a promising collaborative framework for focusing on meaning and the communicative process. The quality of intrinsic, critical thinking and peer support depends on the time allowed for reflection, group experimentation, and holistic language processing. The teacher sets the framework, and students use good literature, their own writing, and authentic oral language. In whole language classrooms, teachers treat students as if they are members of the same literacy club rather than text-bound pupils searching for "correct answers" (Smith, 1985).

Reciprocal Teaching

In reciprocal teaching the teacher and the students take turns playing teacher. This teaching method involves modeling and coaching children in four basic reading comprehension strategies:

1. predicting what will come next
2. formulating questions
3. summarizing what has been read
4. clarifying difficulties in understanding what has been read

Teachers begin by modeling the strategies and then coaching teams of two or more students to take their turn at "teaching" the other teams.

Some student behaviors teachers might want to monitor include whether or not the student:

- shows an interest in words
- turns the pages at the appropriate time
- points to individual words on the page
- notices words and symbols in the environment
- tells a familiar story
- remembers details from a story
- makes up a story
- comments about books read
- reads or looks at books during free time
- uses books as resources
- brings books to class on topics the class is studying
- chooses to read during free time
- compares books, authors or illustrators
- predicts outcomes in stories

Prediction Strategies, Collaboration, and Creative Thinking

Developing readers who can think creatively means teaching students to infer meaning, anticipate story outcomes, discuss higher-level questions, and extrapolate to other situations. In a *directed reading thinking activity* (DRTA) students try to predict ahead on the basis of a few clues that they have been given. As they read they continue to jointly speculate about the story and hypothesize. Divergent responses are encouraged—although opinions must be justified on some logical basis. After the story students demonstrate their understanding by using rather than simply recalling important points. In the early grades predictable books, like *Henny Penny* or *Curious George,* can teach the same kind of thinking and prediction skills. Big books, like those from Scholastic, are particularly useful when reading to younger students. In upper grades a variety of DRTA strategies can be used.

In this sample directed reading thinking activity, pairs of students come up with prediction of what will happen next—and practice reading to the whole group. Students take turns reading the lines and making predictions.

A Sample DRTA:

My big dog went down to the supermarket
What do you think he did?

He stood up, leaned against the window and looked in.
What did he see?
A leg of lamb.... What did he do?

He jumped in and grabbed the leg of lamb.
What did he do with it?

He ran for home.... The police saw him.
What did they do?

They chased him, red lights flashing.
I had just gotten home from work and I heard a knock on the door. Who was it?

It was the police. What did they say?

"Is he yours?...just the facts."

"Yes...." "Do you know he just broke into the supermarket and stole a leg of lamb?

I asked, them, "How do you know you have the right dog?"

Police: "He's chewing the evidence."
What happened next?

I got a $365 bill from Allstate Insurance.
But did they ever bill me for the leg of lamb?

No, but for that price I could get a side of beef.

Collaborative directed thinking and reading activities can be a positive influence as we move from the traditional emphasis on reading skills to a

collaborative literature approach emphasizing creativity and critical thinking skills. Critical and creative thinking abilities relate to making inferences
about daily and special events. These skills might be thought of as
reasonable reflective thinking that is focused on deciding what to believe or
do (Ennis, 1987).

When mixed ability reading and writing groups are used in combination,
directed writing and thinking activities (DWTA) can serve as a vehicle for
allowing ideas to come to fruition and for helping others decide where to go
with their stories. Reading good literature serves as a resource for seeing
how adult writers go about setting the scene for more elaborate presentation
of ideas. The research suggests that collaboratively reading and writing
together prompts more critical thinking and imaginative storytelling (Marcel & Carpenter, 1987). Directly connecting reading and writing programs
also proved effective in achieving multiple perspectives and a greater depth
of understanding (Weintrab, 1988).

Reading activities can include have partners read to each other, make
predictions based on visual (or written) clues, or jointly construct summaries after reading the story. Peer conferences can occur during the
planning, revision, and editing process. Cooperative groups of four to six
help students learn to listen, question, resolve conflicts, share resources, and
make decisions. Group support can also increase the risk taking that is so
important in language learning. In cooperative groups much of the responsibility for learning is placed where it belongs, on the students.

Reading Newspapers for Group Discussion and Writing

With upper grades, middle school, and high school students newspaper
articles cans park ideas for group discussion and provide writing models for
analysis. Students can see how a composition is organized as they read,
rather than watch television. They can also compare the evening news,
which is often based on items in national newspapers with written stories.
The *New York Times,* the *Washington Post,* the *Los Angeles Times,* or the local
newspaper can be more stimulating than textbooks. With younger students
the *Weekly Reader* can replace the adult newspaper.

*Connecting the Newspaper to TV News: The Newspaper Scavenger
Hunt.* The daily newspaper, particularly if it's in a second language, can
be an intimidating document for students to tackle. It is imposing in
format and vocabulary for early readers who are accustomed to materials
geared toward their competency levels. By preparing imaginative exercises using a newspaper and a taped news broadcast, a teacher can
provide an introduction and demystify those pages filled with newsprint
and connect to a second language video segment.

It is important the newspaper and video segment cover some of the same ground. The TV news items or conversations should shown first, so that what the students have listen to (and seen) is then applied to print. This means using print and video material from the same day.

The Newspaper Scavenger Hunt is an exercise that can be applied to a variety of reading levels. A list is drawn up with columns of words and phrases extracted from a sample paper. This list of cartoons, pictures, words, concepts, and short phrases (to be found in the newspaper) is handed out to the students along with the paper. They are then asked to begin the hunt: Students put the page number which the item in the newspaper. A time limit is set for the search to take place. When time is up, the students can compare their "success" rates. This exercise can be modified for a range of ability levels.

The teacher can go over the newspaper with them as the class collaboratively searches for connections with the news program. An additional application could involve making up a creative story composed almost entirely of headlines and subheadings.

Critical Thinking and Improving Reading Comprehension

Another example of a directed reading thinking activity is the inductive-reasoning grid presented here. Students are asked to read, record data, and make inferences about what they read.

Inductive Reasoning Grid

Name of character _____

Reading Clues: *Interpretation:*

1. Statements by the character:

———————————————   ———————————————

———————————————   ———————————————

2. Character's actions:

———————————————   ———————————————

———————————————   ———————————————

3. Character's thinking patterns:

———————————————   ———————————————

———————————————   ———————————————

4. What others say about this
   character:

   _____   _____

   _____   _____

5. Situations the character becomes
   involved in:

   _____   _____

   _____   _____

6. Other important information
   about the character:

   _____   _____

   _____   _____

Summary of the character   *My generalizations about the
                                    character:*

Using Quotes To Spark Collaborative Writing

> *The results of using literature as a base for the reading program are evident . . . If you
> want a child to learn about cats and dogs then put him in a room with a thousand cats
> and a thousand dogs.*
> —Kenneth Goodman

Good writing has more to do with reading good literature and writing a lot
than it does with any collection of rules. Improving communication and
social skills is a goal that can be reached through critical thinking,
innovative thought, concern for the audience, and the realization that the
group swims or sinks together. It's important for students to encourage each
other to read more fully and critically, so that they can write less
simplistically (Perfetti, 1985).

The ideas that follow are offered as suggestions to promote thinking
collaboratively and critically about the writing process.

1. *Sharing Quotes in the prewriting process:*
   Share a quote at your student's level and ask them to respond to it.

   • "Writing, like life itself, is a voyable of discovery."—Henry MIller
   • "Poems are like dreams, you put into them what you don't know
     you know."—A. Rich

- "Writing and rewriting are a constant search for what one is saying."—J. Updike
- "A writer keeps surprising himself... he doesn't know what he is saying until he sees it on the page."—T. Williams
- "One of the reasons a writer writes, I think, is that his stories reveal so much he never thought he knew."—C. Holland
- "The relationship of talk to writing is central to the writing process."—J. Britton
- "Writing a play is thinking, not thinking about thinking."—R. Bolt
- "Writing has got to be an act of discovery
  I write to find out what I'm thinking about."—E. Albee
- "How do I know what I think until I see what I say?"—E. M. Forester

2. *Using Embedded Quotes in Group Writing Projects*
Try focusing on ways to use embedded quotes in personal responses—or quote to support visual imagery. Some samples to encourage students to encourage students to think about the writing process:

- "experimenting in composing with words is experimenting in composing understanding, in composing knowledge. A writer, in a sense, composes the world in which he or she lives."—K. Dowst
- "A painter takes the sun and makes it into a yellow spot. An artist take a yellow spot and makes it into a sun."—Pablo Picasso
- The cold war now belongs to the age of political dinosaurs... The U.S. and the Soviet Union have both been diminished as major powers... The worst effect (in the United States) has been a neglect of democratic reform, a deterioration of basic services, the undermining of confidence in government, and a weakening of the public culture."—C. Lasch
- "An essential part of the writing process is explaining the matter to oneself."—J. Britton
- "Writing usually begins in the self and the composing process is, in part, a search for appropriate modes of approach to an audience. The writer relates his work to his own experience; he must develop this thought on the basis of what he knows."—B. Peterson
- The printed word has contributed significantly to our conception of the self as separate from others and of communication as something other than communion. The simple act of reading, in other words, removes us from direct experience—and frequently from the necessity for it.—P. Williams.
- "Far from doing away with paper, the computer has made all trees in their vicinity quake in terror."—D. Adams

If students connect their personal lives to events in literature, writing and literature can be a window on the world—or on oneself. Quality literature and writing can be approached with a sense of discovery. Having peers and the teacher give feedback to students is a key to improving cooperative behavior. For students, one of the most frequently mentioned cooperative group pleasures is sharing different points of view and combining group ideas (Hartse, Short, & Burke, 1988).

3. *Steps for Developing Young Writers and Readers*
   - Provide models of how experienced writer and readers work in real life.
   - Give student hands-on experiences that help them understand what they write and read.
   - Scale back the use of the basal.
   - Monitor reading and writing development and teach skills in the context of actual reading and writing.
   - Share reading and writing experiences.
   - Create a literacy environment and arrange for small mixed-ability grouping.
   - Spend a large portion of class time actually reading and writing.
   - Build lessons on the background knowledge and experience of the students.
   - Integrates peaking and listening with reading and writing.
   - Facilitate small cooperative group discussions—shift groups to respond to group interests (Adams, 1980).

WRITING IN COLLABORATIVE GROUPS

Groups of between four and six student can generate ideas by brainstorming, discussing issues in the news, or sharing a book they have read during the prewriting process. Listening to new ideas can help pairs of students draft possibilities than contribute to the overall group writing project. After the material has been developed by individuals or pairs, it can be brought together for revision. Here students can exchange drafts and solve overall writing problems by focusing on specific elements.

Writing is not just for language arts or English class. It is an art of creative thinking that can enliven the arts, mathematics, social studies, and the sciences. The give-and-take of writing with peers helps students learn subject matter across the curriculum (Graves, 1983). As children critique each other's writing, it improves. As students compare short essays to explain the solution of a problem or simply write in personal journals, they are able to collaboratively focus on thinking (Dyson, 1989).

Word-processing programs can facilitate the writing process. Using the computer, children can select their topics, write drafts, interact with peers, revise, edit, and publish their work for real audiences. The research suggests that rich social interactions can occur around the computer screen (Cochran-Smith, Kahn, & Paris, 1988; Mehan, 1989).

By turning their language arts classrooms into collaborative ventures, teachers find that students are more willing to select their own topics and explore subjects of real interest to them (Gere, 1985). Drawing on ideas from class, their personal lives, and reading serves as a powerful catalyst for thinking, learning, and developing the art of writing.

Peer Editing

Peer editing requires comprehension, reasoning, and reflection. To be an effective evaluator, student editors should come to a piece of writing with specific questions in mind. The questions on the following checklist can be applied to any kind of writing.

1. What is the focus or main idea of the draft?
2. Are the supporting details related directly to this focus?
3. What additional details should the writer add?
4. Does the draft have a clear organization?
5. Is there anything I find confusing?
6. Are there any awkward or unclear sentences or paragraphs?
7. What do I think or feel after reading the draft? Are these the effects the writer intended?
8. What do I like best about the draft?

Peer editors should keep these points in mind:

- Be sensitive to the writer's feelings and needs. Be courteous.
- Point out strengths as well as weaknesses.
- Supply constructive criticism. Offer suggestions for improvement.
- Focus on ideas and form rather than proofreading.

Most of the editing can be left to the students—sentence structure, paragraphing, or which paper is to go first, second, or third in the final group product. This has proven a better learning process than simply having the teacher collect the first draft and suggest revisions (Hansen, 1987).

To learn to write, children need to know adults who write. So modeling behavior on the part of the teacher is important (Perfetti, 1985). Besides working with their peers, students need to see the teacher in the process of composing. And they need to see the messy drafts as the teacher moves toward the final product. Writing is a process that involves prewriting, drafting, revising, editing and sharing. It is a tool to be used across the curriculum.

ASSESSMENT

Processing and Thinking About Written Expression

It's important to emphasize the need for a *community* of writers, because it is a powerful way to help *individuals* develop (Heilbrun, 1989). Whether writing is self-, peer, or teacher evaluated, it is important not to lose sight of the connection between what is valued and what is valuable. Jointly developed folders (portfolios) have a major role to play in student writing assessment by providing a running record of what a child can and can't do. The selection that follows offers criteria and descriptions for another type of assessment.

To work toward less control, teachers need to help students take more responsibility for their own learning. The ability to evaluate does not come easily at first, and peer writing groups will need teacher-developed strategies to help them process what they have learned. The ability to reflect on being a member of peer writing team is a form of metacognition—learning to think about thinking, and changing behavior as a result (Gardner, 1987). This requires processing in a circular or U-shaped group where all students can see each other. Questions for evaluative processing might include:

- How did group leadership evolve?
- Was it easy to get started?
- How did you feel if one of your ideas was left out?
- What did you do if most members of your group thought that you should write something differently?
- How did you rewrite?
- Did your paper say what you wanted it to?
- What kind of a setting do you like for writing?
- How can you arrange yourself in the classroom to make the writing process better?
- What writing tools did you use?
- How do you feel when you write?

Teachers can ask themselves whether or not students use reading and writing for:

- personal expression
- organizing new insights

- participating in the culture
- demonstrating knowledge
- thinking critically
- developing interpersonal skills
- demonstrating literacy competence

Holistic Grading of Written Expression

This process is now a major way to grade written experiences—from the elementary school through college. It involves looking at how the overall concepts are devoleped instead of concentrating on mechanical errors (Johnson, 1989). This can be used with a student's writing portfolio. When students learn to maintain portfolios of their work, they can learn to assess their progress and the progress of peers (Johnson, 1989). Writing portfolios can include holistic scores of peers and teachers on writing samples, and work samples of final drafts of the writing process. When this is done, students, teachers, and parents can look over a student's writing history and assess the range and fluidity of the students' compositions.

Criteria for Holistic Scoring.

Grades 5/6   Clearly above-average papers that demonstrate strength in virtually all the criteria. Rarely are these flawless papers, but they are usually substantial in content and often original in idea and/or expression A "5" tends to be thinner or weaker in some ways than a clearly "6" (superior). For example, if third graders are asked to write about how to build a swing, you could actually do it from this paper.

Grades 3/4   Papers ranging from slightly below average ("3") to slightly above average ("4"), either combining strengths with weaknesses in the various criteria or showing an over-all sense of under-development. (The swing might get built if you read this paper.)

Grades 1/2   Clearly below average papers which fail to demonstrate competence on several of the criteria (often because the paper is too short) or which are generally empty or which fail to respond to the question. A "2" tends to have redeeming qualities absent in a "1." (There is little chance that someone could build anything from this one.)

Grade 0   Papers which are *wholly* off topic. Such papers neither state nor imply that a change of any kind has taken place. (It's about paper airplanes, rather than swing building.)

Other assessment concerns might focus on portfolios—those reading and writing activities actually occurring in the classroom. Questions might focus on:

- How well were the students able to communicate their ideas through writing?
- How well did they use the composing strategies of planning, drafting, revising, and editing?
- What collaborative strategies did students use for getting help with their reading and writing?
- How well were students able to use the reading strategies of guiding, monitoring, adapting, and responding to what was being read? (Johnson, 1987)

Sample Writing Stimulus

If you think about it, you're really not the same person you were 4 or 5 years ago. Your ideas, tastes, attitudes, and perhaps even your goals have changed—probably in several ways. Choose any one person (a relative, a teacher, a friend, or anyone else) or any event or experience (a course, a trip, a conversation, or any other event or experience) that has made a difference in your life, and explain as fully as you can how the person or event has changed you. Be as specific as you can in showing how you are different now because of the person or event. In writing your composition, be aware of the following elements:

ideas —The extent to which the thoughts and content of the essay are original, insightful, and clear

supporting —The extent to which the ideas of the essay are supported by examples and details which are specific, appropriate, original, and well developed.

unity —The extent to which the parts of the essay are connected to each other and all help achieve the goal of the essay.

style —The extent to which the language of the essay is used creatively and correctly and helps achieve the writer's goals.

In most informed assessment of writing pupils are asked to produce a written sample. Then the student's peers or teacher looks at:

1. *fluency* —A measure that involves factors such as length of sentences. In general, the longer the sentences tend to be, the higher the fluency.

2. *sentence types*   —Are they fragmented? The goal is to combine sentence fragments and vary the type.

3. *vocabulary*   —Are the words limited or does the student make good use of unusual words in a passage?

4. *structure, sequence, and grammar*   —Important in the final product.

5. *ideas*   —Are they interesting, original, and to the point?

POETRY AND COLLABORATION

Poetry is not just "bad prose." To read or write it involves awareness of certain elements that make it unique. Teachers must have some basic knowledge of the vocabulary of poetry in order to help children enjoy and mature in their understanding and appreciation of it (Hollander, 1989). Some characteristics include:

1. Poetry uses condensed language; every word is important.
2. Poetry uses figurative language (e.g., metaphor, simile, personification, irony)
3. The language of poetry is rhythmical (regular, irregular, metered).
4. Some words may be rhymed (internal, end of line, run-over) or nonrhyming.
5. Poetry uses the language of sounds (alliteration, assonance, repetition).
6. The units or organization are line arrangements in stanzas or idea arrangements in story, balance, contrast, build-up, surprise, and others.
7. Poetry uses the language of imagery (sense perceptions reproductions in the mind) (Denman, 1989).

Different Kinds of Poetry

1. *Fixed Forms*
    a. Narrative or storytelling
    b. Literary forms with prescribed structures (e.g., limerick, ballad, sonnet, haiku, others)
    c. Lyric
2. *Free Verse*
    a. Tone: humorous, serious, nonsensical, sentimental, dramatic, didactic
    b. Content: humor, nonsense, everyday things, animals, seasons, family, fantasy, people, feelings, adventure, moods
    c. Time of Writing: contemporary, traditional (Nell, 1989).

3. *An Example of Collaborative Poetry*

    Students work in small collaborative groups. Each team is given a short time (one or two minutes) to compose the first line of a poem. On a signal from the teacher, each team passes their paper to the next group and receives one from another. The group reads the line that the preceding team has written and adds a second line. The signal is given and the papers rotate again—each time the group reads and adds a second line. The signal is given and the papers rotate again—each time the group reads and adds another line. Teams are encouraged to write what comes to mind, even if it's only their name. They must write something in the time allotted. After 8 or 10 lines the papers are returned to their original team. Groups can add a line if they choose, revise and edit the poem they started. The poems can then be read orally, with team members alternating reading the lines. Later, some of them can be turned into an optic poem (creating a picture with computer graphics using the words of the poem) or acted out using ribbons or penlights (while someone else reads the poem).

Experiences With Poetry

1. *Poetry with Movement and Music*

    Poems can be put to music and movement. Students can also illustrate picture books or poems to share with younger children.

2. *Daily Oral Reading of Poetry*

    Students sign up and read aloud at the end of each day. Other students "point," commenting on parts of the poem that catch their attention. A classroom anthology of poetry can be illustrated and laminated.

3. *Responding During Free Writing Period*

    Thirty minutes to an hour and one-half are set aside each day for students to write on any topic, in whatever form they choose. A share time follows so that other students may respond to each other's writing by pointing and asking questions.

4. *Literature Share Time*

    Students gather in small groups once a week to share books they have been reading. The groups are structured so that each student
    a. reads the author and title of each book
    b. tells about the book
    c. reads one or two pages aloud
    d. receives responses from members of the group, specifically pointing out parts they liked and asking questions.

5. *Wish Poems*

    Each student writes a wish on a strip of paper. The wishes are read together as a whole for the group. Students then write individual wish poems which are shared.

6. *Group Metaphor Comparisons*
   Poems containing metaphors are read aloud. Group comparison poems
   are written on the board. Students write individual comparison poems
   and share them with the class.
7. *Sample Poetry Lesson*
   A lesson developed from *Dinosaurs,* a poetry anthology for children
   edited by Lee Bennett Hopkins.
   a. Teacher reads poems aloud.
   b. Students brainstorm reasons why the dinosaurs died, and words
      that relate to how the dinosaurs moved.
   c. Models of dinosaurs and pictures are displayed and talked about.
   d. Students write poems and share them.

CREATIVE DRAMA AND COLLABORATION

Creative drama can make important contributions to children's literacy
development (Johnson, Christie, & Yawkey, 1987). Engaging in literacy-
related creative drama should be part of every language arts program. These
activities can be done in small groups with few props and no memorization
of lines, and are free from the risk of failure. Dramatic play can be used to
bridge the gap between written and visual forms of communication. For
example, students can work in small groups to script, act, and even
videotape a 1-minute commercial. They can then critically examine the
reasoning behind each group's presentation to the class. Activities can be as
simple as picking a topic and deciding how the group will present it,
practice the skit, and perform it for the class.

Creative Drama.

- Doesn't emphasize performance.
- Adapts to many types of books, lessons, and subjects.
- Encourages the clarification of values.
- Evokes contributions and responses from students who rarely participate
  in "standard" discussions.
- Evaluates, in English classes, how well students know the material
  (characterization, setting, plot, conflicts).
- Provides a stimulating prewriting exercise.

Creative dramatics emphasizes four fundamental educational objectives:

1. provides for self realization in unified learning experiences
2. offers first hand experiences in democratic behavior
3. provides functional learning which is related to life
4. contributes to comprehensive learning (Cazden, 1988).

Teaching Story Dramatization.

1. Select a good story—and then tell it to the group.
2. With the class, break the plot down into sequences, or scenes, that can be acted out.
3. Have groups select a scene they wish to dramatize.
4. Instruct the groups to break the scene or scenes into further sequence, and discuss the setting, motivation, characterizations, roles, props, etc. Encourage students to get involved in the developmental images of the characters—what they did, how they did it, why they did it. Have groups make notes on their discussions.
5. Meet with groups to review and discuss their perceptions. Let them go into conference and plan in more detail for their dramatization.
6. Have the whole class meet back together and watch the productions of each group. Instruct students to write down five things they liked and five things that could be improved in the next playing.
7. Let the players return to their groups at the end of all group performances and evaluate the dramas using the criteria in number 6.
8. Allow groups to bring back their group evaluations to the whole class. Discuss findings, suggestions, and positive group efforts.

Reminders and Pointers.

1. Do not rush students. Side coach if necessary; examples: "Take your time." "You're doing fine."
2. Try to keep an environment where each can find his or her own nature without imposition. Growth is natural to everyone.
3. A group of individuals who act, agree, and share together create strength and release knowledge surpassing the contribution of any single member.
4. If, during sessions, students become restless and static in their work, it is a danger sign. Refreshment and a new focus is needed.
5. Become familiar with the many resource and game books useful in this work.
6. Be flexible. Alter your plans on a moment's notice.
7. While a team is performing, the teacher must observe audience reactions as well as the play work. The interaction of the audience is part of the creative dramatics experience.
8. Avoid giving examples. Too often the students become bound to that example and don't try new things.
9. If the environment in the workshop is joyous and free of authoritarianism, everyone will "play" and become as open as young children.

Creative Drama with Active Learning Teams

1. *Personification: A Prewriting Activity*
   Each student draws the name of an inanimate object (pencil sharpener, doorknob, waste basket, alarm clock, etc.) Students pick a partner and develop an improvisation.

2. *Showing Emotions*
   Assign a "emotion" to each student (anger, jealousy, shyness, nervousness, nerdiness, arrogance, etc.) Students must act out the emotion without actually naming or referring to it. The class notes significant details and discusses which emotion was being portrayed.

3. *Using Drama To Extend a Story*
   Creative drama can extend a story. Try "blocking" a play as you read it aloud in class. Giving a visual perspective increases concentration.

4. *Increasing Research and Journalism Skills*
   Using techniques of role playing and creative drama, have student groups show *how* to interview (give good and bad examples). Short excerpts from TV news or radio information programs provide good models for discussion and creative drama activities.

5. *Using Creative Drama to Increase Vocabulary*
   Assign five words to a group and let them use them in a skit.

6. *Creating Character Transpositions*
   Students can imagine the story they have just read in a town or city that they have seen. Take a character from some historical period and present him or her with a dilemma of the 1990s. Design a skit around one of these situations.

   The King Arthur Tales:

   — Merlin working in a used car lot.
   — Lancelot at a rock concert.
   — Guenivere at a NOW meeting.
   — Arthur interviewing for a job on Wall Street

7. *Redefining History: Sending Students Back Through Time...*
   The Crucible

   — What happens to a 1990s teenager (with Walkman & black T-shirt) who somehow lands in Salem at the height of the witch hysteria?

Within these activities students can be viewed as performers required to demonstrate their collective knowledge. The teacher's role is like that of a coach—helping students know and interpret the standards provoking thought.

Literacy and Creative Thinking

Creative drama and writing are good ways for students to share imaginative ideas with their peers creating an atmosphere where unconscious thought can flow freely. Exploring how community or historical figures developed their ability to think imaginatively can help. The following are elements to look for in creative thinking:

*Fluency	— Producing and considering many alternatives.
*Originality	— Producing ideas which go beyond the obvious and are unique and valued.
*Highlighting the essence:	— Finding and expressing the main idea.
*Elaboration:	— Filling out an idea or set of ideas by adding details.
*Keeping Open:	— Delaying closure, seeing many ideas, considering a rang e of information, making mental leaps.
*Awareness of Emotions	— Developing and expressing emotional awareness, perseverance, involvement, and commitment.
*Combining and Synthesizing:	— Seeing relationships and joining parts and elements to form a whole.
*Visualizing—Richly and Colorfully:	— Perceiving and creating images which are vivid, strong and alive.
*Visualizing— The Inside:	— Seeing and presenting ideas and objects from an internal vantage point.
*Enjoying and Using Fantasy	— Making use of imagination in a playful way.
*Using Movement:	— Learning, thinking, and communicating kinesthetically.
*Using Sound	— Interpreting and communicating ideas, concepts, and feelings through sound and music.
*Breaking through and Extending Boundaries:	— Overcoming limitations and conventions, and creating new solutions.
*Using Humor	— Combining incongruous situations with comical wit, surprise, and amusement.

*Imagining the Future — Envisioning alternatives, predicting consequences, and planning ahead.

Students learn elements of creative thinking from interpersonal group behaviors. Cooperative groups can help develop these and other language skills in a variety of ways: listening, speaking, arguing, problem solving, and clarifying. So does having pairs of students argue an issue with other pairs, then switching sides. The chaos and dissonance of group work can actually foster critical thinking and imaginative language development. This way students learn to work creatively with conflicts, viewing them as possibilities for the cooperative improvement of literacy.

Literacy and Social Interaction

Children's language learning and social interaction must go together.
—Vygotsky

The literacy skills of the American public are the lowest in the industrialized world. It is important to consider why this society has been inhospitable to certain social and educational possibilities. The result of high levels of illiteracy are not only hazardous for those affected but for the country as a whole (Chall, Jacobs, & Baldwin, 1990). Many political leaders and business executives have urged the investment of as much economic, political and educational capital as needed to overhaul American schools. As economist Sue Berryman has noted

The well educated face of a future of expanding job opportunities and rising wages, while those not well educated face a future of contracting opportunities and poverty.

What can be done to improve our literacy rates? All children deserve the same kind of supportive environment at school that has served literary growth at home. This means interacting with meaningful stories to accomplish genuine purposes. The goal of adult mediation should be to provide information that students need to know when they need to know it. It is parents and teachers who must create a literate environment and mediate the learning that goes on by modeling the use of literacy activities. Some teachers meet with parents before school starts to set cooperative goals and ask parents about the child's strong and weak points—what works for him or her, and what doesn't. Parents can make a big contribution to their child's success in school.

When teachers change their methods and classroom organizational structures, they need the cooperation of administrators, parents, and teacher educators. Along with reading print, writing, and creative language experiences goes developing the capacity for aesthetic response and making sure that literacy instruction is a satisfying experience for all learners (Cooper, 1988).

Collaborative language inquiry can provide children with a sense of efficacy. Literacy development requires intrinsically motivating activities that help students develop the right habits of the mind. Engaging youngsters in an active group exploration of ideas is exciting and fun. For the seeds of literacy to grow, teachers must take themselves seriously as agents of change who arrange classroom environments for cooperation and engagement, and provide for the needs of all children.

The greatest thing in this world is not so much where we are, but in what direction we are going.
    —Oliver Wendell Holmes

REFERENCES

Adams, D. (1980). *Sparks for learning*. Watertown, MA: ESN Press.

Ashton, P.T., & Rodman, B.W. (1986). *Making a difference: Teachers sense of efficacy and student achievement*. New York: Longman.

Bruffee, K.A. (1984). Collaborative learning and the conversation of mankind. *College English, 46,* 635-652.

Burns, P., Roe, B., & Ross, E. (1988). *Teaching reading in today's elementary schools*. Boston: Houghton Mifflin.

Cazden, C. (1988). *Classroom discourse: The language of teaching and learning*. Portsmouth, NH: Heineman.

Chall, J., Jacobs, B., & Baldwin, L. (1990). *The reading crisis*. Cambridge, MA: Harvard University Press.

Cochran-Smith, M., Kahn, J., & Paris, C.L. (1988). When word processors come into the classroom. In J.L. Hoot & S.B. Silvern (Eds.), *Writing with computers in the early grades*. New York: Teachers College Press.

Conley, M. (1987). *Grouping within reach*. Newark, DE: International Reading Association.

Cooper, C.R. (Ed.). (1988). *Researching response to literature and the teaching of literature*. Norwood, NJ: Ablex Publishing Corp.

Denman, G. (1989). *When you've made it your own . . . : Teaching poetry to young people*. Portsmouth, NH: Heinemann Educational Books.

Dyson, A.H. (1989). *The multiple worlds of child writers: A study of friends learning to write*. New York: Teachers College Press.

Ennis, R. (1987). A taxonomy of critical thinking dispositions and abilities. In J. Boyokoff Baron & R. Sternberg (Eds.), *Teaching thinking skills: Theory and practice*. New York: W.H. Freeman & Co.

Flood, J., & Lapp, D. (Eds.). (1989). *Instructional theory and practice for content area reading and learning.* Englewood Cliffs, NJ: Prentice-Hall.

Gardner, R. (1987). *Metacognition and reading comprehension.* Norwood, NJ: Ablex Publishing Corp.

Gere, A.R. (Ed.). (1985). *Roots in the sawdust: Writing to learn across the disciplines.* Urbana, IL: National Council of Teachers of English.

Graves, D. (1983). *Writing, teachers and children at work.* Exeter, NH: Heineman.

Hansen, J. (1987). *When writers read.* Portsmouth, NH: Heineman.

Hartse, J., Short, K., & Burke, C. (1988). *Creating classrooms for authors.* Portsmouth, NH: Heinemann.

Heilbrun, C. (1989). *Writing a woman's life.* New York: Norton.

Hollander, J. (1989). *Melodious guile: Fictive pattern in poetic language.* New Haven, CT: Yale University Press.

Johnson, J.E., Christie, J.F., & Yawkey, T. (1987). *Play and early childhoood development.* Glenview, IL: Scott Foresman.

Johnson, K. (1987). *Doing words: Using the creative power of children's personal images to teach reading and writing.* Boston: Houghton Mifflin.

Johnson, P.H. (1989, April 7). Teachers as evaluation experts: A cognitive basis. *The Reading Teacher,* pp. 44-48.

Linfors, J. (1987). *Children's language and learning.* Englewood Cliffs, NJ: Prentice-Hall.

Marcel, A., & Carpenter, P. (1987). *The psychology of reading and language comprehension.* Newton, MA: Allyn and Bacon.

Mehan, H. (1989). Microcomputers in classrooms: Educational technology or social practice? *Anthropology and Education Quarterly, 20*(1), 4-22.

Nagy, W.E. (1988). *Teaching vocabulary to improve reading comprehension.* Urbana, IL: National Council of Teachers of English.

Nell, V. (1989). *Lost in a book.* New Haven, CT: Yale University Press.

Perfetti, C. (1985). *Reading ability.* New York: Oxford University Press.

Resnick, L. (1987). *Education and learning to think: 1987 report.* Washington, DC: National Academy Press.

Short, K.G., & Burke, C.L. (1988). *Creating curricula which foster thinking.* Urbana, IL: National Council of Teachers of English.

Smith, F. (1985). *Reading without nonsense.* New York: Teachers College Press.

Solomon, P., & Claire, H. (1984). *Classroom collaboration.* London: Routledge & Kagan.

Vygotsky, L. (1986). *Thought and language.* Cambridge, MA: MIT Press.

Weintraub, S. (Ed.). (1988). *Summary of investigations relating to reading.* Newark, DE: International Reading Association.

4

SCIENTIFIC LITERACY

Extending Collaboration Through Science, Numeracy, and Mathematics

Scientific illiteracy in general—and innumeracy in particular—are social ills created by increased demand for the applications of numbers and scientific concepts.
—Paulos

Scientific literacy encompasses science, mathematics, and technology. Although it has emerged as a major theme in American educational reform, it remains an elusive goal. Numerous studies have made it clear that U.S. education is failing too many students in this area—and thus failing the country. But are we really quite as bad off as everyone seems to think?

In a recent public opinion study, less than half of American adults knew that the earth annually revolves around the sun, astronomy was confused with astrology, and two in five believed alien creatures have visited the earth (Miller, 1990). At least pseudoscience is doing well.

International comparisons rank American fifth graders 8th out of 17 countries in science achievement. By ninth-grade U.S. students are in 15th place (out of 17). Even advanced placement high school physics students scored 9th and advanced chemistry students 11th in a 13-country comparison. Results on mathematics tests are similar. American eighth-grade students scored well below other countries in solving problems that require analysis and higher levels of thinking (National Assessment of Educational Progress, 1989).

The precarious state of science and mathematics learning for black and Hispanic youth is also disturbing. At ages 13 and 17 minority students perform four or more years behind their white counterparts. In addition to these problems, recent surveys by the U.S. Education Department found that a majority of girls, disadvantaged students, and minorities were lost to science and mathematics by the time they left elementary school; lack of effective instruction and loss of student interest were cited as the major culprits in this loss of talent (Clewell, 1987).

America has an urgent priority in reforming science, mathematics, and technology education. In the next 10 years, an estimated 70% of jobs will be related somehow to the technology of computers, numeracy, and electronics. Business leaders, public officials, and teachers argue that, without solid skills in these areas, students will not be prepared for even the most routine work. Also the United States will lack the science and engineering talent to compete effectively in the global market. Worse yet, the nature of our democracy is threatened by ill-informed voters unable to make decisions about issues critical to the welfare of this country and the global community.

The evidence suggests we *are* as bad off as everyone thinks.

Scientific Literacy

Knowledge of science, mathematics, and technology is valuable for everyone, because it makes the world more understandable and more interesting. All students should have an awareness of what the scientific endeavor is and how it relates to their culture and their lives. This means understanding the union of science, mathematics, and technology, its roots, the human contributions, and its limitations, as well as its miracles. Recognizing the role of the scientific endeavor and how science, mathematics, and technology interact with society is one of the basic dimensions of scientific literacy. The National Council on Science and Technology Education identifies a *scientifically literate* person as one who:

- recognizes the diversity and unity of the natural world.
- understands the important concepts and principles of science.
- is aware of the ways that science, mathematics, and technology depend on each other.
- knows that mathematics, science, and technology are human endeavors and recognizes what this implies about the strengths and weaknesses of science, mathematics, and technology.
- has a capacity for scientific ways of thinking.
- makes use of scientific knowledge and ways of thinking in personal and social interactions (American Association for the Advancement of Science, 1990).

Scientific literacy also includes seeing scientific endeavors through the perspective of cultural and intellectual history and becoming familiar with ideas that cut across subject lines. This involves an awareness that most of the scientific views held today resulted from many small discoveries over time and are a product of cultural and historical ways of thinking and viewing the world. Significant historical events such as Galileo's perspective on the earth's place in the universe; Newton's discoveries of laws of motion; Darwin's observations of diversity, variety, and evolving life forms; and Pasteur's identification of infections disease stemming from microscopic organisms are milestones in the development of Western thought and events.

People have always been concerned with transmitting attitudes, shared values, and ways of thinking to the next generation. Today it seems more critical as every part of contemporary life is bombarded by science and technology. Part of scientific literacy consists of clarifying attitudes, possessing certain scientific values, and making informed judgments. Students need to cultivate scientific patterns of thinking, logical reasoning, curiosity, an openness to new ideas, and skepticism in evaluating claims and arguments.

Positive attitudes are also important. Being able to understand the basic principles of science, being "numerate" in dealing with quantitative matters, thinking critically, measuring accurately, using ordinary tools of science and mathematics (including calculators and computers), are all part of the scientific literacy equation.

To achieve this type of scientific literacy, students need to be able to:

- develop and apply creative and rational thinking abilities
- develop values and attitudes that promote ethical and moral thinking
- develop a perspective that promotes the interdependent nature of the environment and global society
- develop the ability for holistic thinking
- develop ability to use science concepts, facts, and principles in the solution of problems
- manipulate the materials of science and communicate science and mathematics information.

Numeracy

Numeracy is to mathematics as literacy is to language
—Steen

Scientific literacy also includes numeracy. *Numeracy* is defined as "those mathematical skills which enable an individual to cope with the practical demands of everyday life" (Cockcroft, 1986). Most of us put many mathematical skills to use every day. The ability to compare costs, understand graphs, calculate risks, estimate distances, and appreciate the effects of the deficit reflect the different dimensions in which mathematics and statistical ideas operate. No matter what one's job or standard of living, numeracy skills are directly linked to informed, confident decision making. Those who lack confidence or skills lead their lives at the mercy of others. Advertisers, lotteries, or dishonest individuals "after a buck" prey on those who avoid examining exaggerated quantitative claims. Without practical numeracy, people are left defenseless against those who would take advantage of their money and good intentions.

Society is also at a disadvantage with innumerate citizens. On issues such as acid rain, the federal budget, global warming, crime, population census, and AIDS, arguments and economics depend in essential ways on aspects of mathematical analyses. Being able to understand how large a billion is, comprehend the probability of winning the lottery, or estimating the likelihood of getting an infectious disease are essential skills. A public unable to reason is an electorate unable to discriminate between reasonable and reckless claims in public policy. Debates ranging from acceptable levels of radiation to waste management require a sophisticated level of numeracy.

The skills required for practical numeracy can be taught to most students during the elementary and middle school years (Silver, 1985). Yet traditional school mathematics programs have concentrated largely on arithmetic. Science teaching has changed little in the last 40 years. In elementary classrooms across the country, science lessons are an hour or so a week of teacher-directed, textbook-driven instruction. Many students don't encounter "real science" until middle or high school. Even then, science is largely fact driven and didactic. Current curricula largely consist of textbooks, teacher talk, and testing. This flies in the face of the fact that there is general agreement that mathematics and science curricula for the 1990s should emphasize thinking skills and model methods of cooperative inquiry (Aronowitz, 1990).

Changing the Image

A new pattern for teaching mathematics and science is emerging which focuses on the nature of learning rather than on the content or method of instruction. It emphasizes relationships and views science and mathematics as a process or a journey. Today's focus is on how to motivate students for life-long learning of science and mathematics, how to awaken curiosity and encourage creativity, rather than how to answer questions correctly or memorize facts. Students are encouraged to relate and apply science to social problems, to mathematics, to technology, to creative innovation, and to their personal lives (National Council of Teachers of Mathematics, 1989).

In the latest approaches science and mathematics are seen as touching people, caring for the planet, and helping students become socially responsible citizens. Today's best science and mathematics teaching emphasizes inquiry and builds on students understandings and misunderstandings. A priority is given to improving students' self-image; self-concept is viewed an indication of performance. Some of the newest methods for teaching science and mathematics include techniques such as creative visualization or mental imagery, keeping daily logs or journals, and expressing attitudes through creative endeavors such as writing, building, or art. Holistic creative thinking is encouraged, as well as projects and presentations that combine experiential knowledge with theoretical understandings. Emphasis is on exciting examples and everyday applications. The student is a participant and an explorer (Paul, Binker, Jensen, & Kreklau, 1989).

Contemporary mathematics recommendations have suggested a broader curriculum including estimation skills, problem solving, practical geometry, statistics, data analysis, calculator skills, probability, measurement, and patterns. The connection of mathematics and science to other subjects, from history to sports, is another objective. Civic, leisure, and cultural features of numeracy and science are rarely discussed or developed in school. All too often math and science are taught as a separate set of skills needed for the next academic level.

Today's students need opportunities to make connections, to work with peers on interesting problems. They also need to be able to apply the skills they are learning to real-life situations (Peterson, 1988). Computational skills, the ability to express basic mathematical understandings, to estimate confidently and check the reasonableness of estimates, are part of what it means to be scientifically literate, numerate, and employable.

Increasingly, school learning is augmented by museum visits, community group meetings, outdoor education programs, peer teaching, and programs for parents. In the cooperative classroom, the science teacher is becoming more of a facilitator and a learner. Students are coming to share in some of the teaching chores. Science is also coming to be seen as part of an interdisciplinary experience where the emphasis is on relating science to the students' world and other subjects.

This kind of teaching has implications for teachers. Some suggestions:

- allow time for creativity and the incubation of ideas, and encourage students to imagine and question
- encourage the use of a variety of materials and sources
- use techniques such as brainstorming to generate ideas, open-ended discussions, collaborating with peers
- involve students in long-term collaborative projects
- integrate science processes and conceptual knowledge in ways that reflect the richness and complexity of science itself.

Examining Learning

Problems in learning mathematics and science are the major reasons why students fail in school. Much of the failure is due to a tradition of teaching that doesn't match the way students learn. Cognitive psychologists, such as Piaget and Bruner, explained long ago how students construct understandings based on their own experiences, and that each individual's knowledge of math and science is personal (Bruner & Haste, 1987). No wonder that computing, listening, and memorizing abstract concepts or symbolic procedures leave a bad taste for the subject.

Worksheets, homework, textbook pages, and repetition may help some students do well on standardized tests. But much of what is memorized is soon forgotten. Lower-order skills are generally ineffective for developing much-needed higher-order thinking and problem-solving abilities. The results are just as bad when students are trained to search for right answers or hints of "how to do the page." Neglecting thinking skills, conceptual understanding, and logical reasoning is neglecting scientific literacy. The true goals of mathematics and science education should be to help students learn how to apply knowledge and solve problems. Students need to be able to use science processes to change their own theories and beliefs in ways that are personally meaningful and consistent with scientific explanations. This way they can develop conceptual understanding and the means for integrating science knowledge into their personal experience.

To really learn science and math, students must construct their own understandings, examine, represent, solve, transform, apply, prove, and communicate. This happens most effectively when they work together in groups to discuss, make presentations, and create their own theories. Such an environment encourages students to engage in a great deal of invention as they impose their interpretation on what is presented and create theories that makes sense to them.

Learning about science and mathematics also involves learning to think critically and create relationships. How these relationships are structured in a student's mind depends on such factors as maturity, physical experience, and social interactions. The ability to inquire, collaborate, and investigate fuels personal autonomy and self-direction in learning. The inability to do these things (scientific illiteracy) leads to inequality of opportunity, weakens our capacity for productive competition, and undermines American civic culture.

Promoting Confidence and Motivation

Research findings continually point out that students need to *feel competent* if they a re going to be motivated to do mathematics and science (NCTM,

1989). Much of the problem with competence is rooted in society's acceptance of poor attitudes about students' potential for success in mathematics and science. It's all too common to hear adults and parents point out, "I was never good in mathematics," or "I was never very interested in science." Yet these same individuals would never admit to being unable to read. These are comparable skills! Poor attitudes about mathematics and science are passed along to children, with accompanying low expectations resulting in low motivation and low levels of achievement.

Motivation is a desire to learn, to explore, to find out, to share with others. To be motivated is to be active, moving, to have high levels of energy and a desire for personal fulfillment. Motivation is not such a big problem for most primary students—they arrive at school with it. Most children have confidence that they are capable and feel good about their performance. Many report mathematics and science to be their favorite subjects. As students spend time in school, this attitude is diminished. By upper grades many students have learned how to look good in relation to others and feel successful when they have beat out their peers. They've developed the ability to monitor their performance and compete—at least on a superficial level. Teachers often encourage such competition. This is sometimes effective for top students who can perform better than their peers. But lower achievers most often feel defeated.

Good experienced teachers are familiar with these problems, so therefore they encourage students to complete a task adequately, regardless of how well other students do. Thus students feel competent when they have learned something new, regardless of what other students have done. In the cooperative classroom competence is based on comparing their new knowledge to knowledge they possessed in the past. This promotes active involvement. All students can feel competent and motivated because they are improving.

A cooperative learning environment provides success and motivation for all students without the external pressures of fear, retribution, or punishment. To help students feel actively involved and thus competent and motivated, teachers can:

1. Use cooperative groups and encourage discussion of mathematics and science. Students should be encouraged to work collaboratively on challenging problems and experiments. Students who work as a team do not worry about their own competence, because success and failure depend on the group as a whole.
2. Let students know that the teacher has confidence in their ability to learn mathematics and science. It is important that students develop a belief that, with a reasonable effort, they can learn. The belief that some people cannot learn math or biology is a myth, popularized by

American society, that must be overcome (Dossey, Mullis, Lindquist, & Chambers, 1988).

3. Praise students effort and performance when it is deserved. Praise for mediocre work gives students the feeling that the teacher doubts that they are capable of anything better. It is often a fine line between encouraging and overpraising.

4. Stress the importance of self improvement over competition or "being the best." Students need to feel that success comes from personal involvement rather than outperforming others. It is better to say "Jane, you did much better today" than "Jane, you did better than Susan."

5. Let students know about the level of difficulty on assignments. A difficult exercise will require more effort, creative thinking, and problem solving. Groups need to feel a level of satisfaction and accomplishment at solving difficult or challenging tasks. Poorly motivated students must be told success results as much from making a good effort as from getting the right answer.

6. Grade on the basis of achievement of objectives rather than on a competitive curve. All students who achieve what they are supposed to, get passing grades. Groups are graded on how well they stuck to the task, worked together, used resources, experimented, tried out strategies, and presented their findings. If they did not arrive at the correct answer after a sincere effort, others should be encouraged to offer assistance, or the group, after consultation with the teacher, may wish to try again rather than get frustrated or discouraged.

7. Stress the usefulness of mathematics and science. Students who believe that learning these subjects is important for success in school and jobs will be more motivated than students who see no purpose or utility for mathematics and science. Discussing careers in science, technology, and mathematics that require numeracy and scientific literacy helps groups see the usefulness of what they are studying.

8. Make connections between mathematics and current problems, environmental issues, recreation, school activities, sports, or any other area of high interest to students.

A Cooperative Learning Perspective

Through our extraordinary ability to question, learn, and above all collaborate with one another, *we have built the remarkable edifice of modern science, which has allowed us to place members of our species on the moon. Yet we are at times both exasperatingly unable to behave rationally and abjectly powerless to solve some of our most pressing medical and social problems. (emphasis added)*
—Robin Dunbar

Learning about math and science is enhanced when students are given opportunities to explain their own ideas, interact with others, explore, question, and try out new approaches. There is substantial evidence that students working in groups can master science and mathematics material better than students working alone (Slavin, 1989). The more opportunities students have for social interaction, the more divergent viewpoints and perspectives can season their thinking. Through collaborative group explorations, students can be pushed to analyze what they think, discuss it, and clarify their own reasoning. Working in small groups also gives students a chance to interact with concepts and verbalize their conceptions within a relatively safe situation. It's often easier to ask questions of our peers. Structuring learning environments where working together is part of the classroom culture encourages more participation with less worry about "being wrong."

As most teachers know from experience, cooperative group work is more than pushing some desks together. Students must have a reason to take one another's progress seriously and care about the team's success. This happens most effectively when students are engaged in active group learning, because everyone takes responsibility for the learning of individual members. This means everyone has a chance to use equipment and manipulate materials to help solve the problem. Cooperative learning means that suggestions from low-achieving students are not to be pushed aside because they interfere with efficiency. Active cooperation is different. Rather than having group success based on a single product, it is the sum of individual learning performances of all members. Collaborative goals are based on *all* group members learning and *doing*.

A Cooperative Learning Model for Conceptual Change

Cognitive views of learning that emphasize prior knowledge and thinking processes within the learner suggest that changes need to be made in the ways that educators think about learners, teaching, and organizing the school classroom (Garofalo, 1988). Research on teaching and learning in science and mathematics suggests that science is most meaningful to learners when it is useful in making sense of the world they encounter (Champagne & Klopfer, 1988). Concepts are best understood when students can apply them to a variety of situations. This means that students need chances to criticize a science experiment and do graphic calculations. They also need to explore aspects of our society that tend to encourage (or inhibit) scientific progress, and investigate technological advances that have been based on work of persons of several races or nationalities.

Central to creating such a learning environment is the desire to help individuals collaboratively acquire or construct knowledge. The underlying concept is that knowledge is to be shared or developed—rather than held by the authority. This holds teachers to a high standard, for they must have subject matter knowledge and a high level of pedagogical expertise that's based on an understanding of cognitive and developmental processes.

The cooperative learning model for science and math suggests that the intrinsic benefits of learning are more important than external rewards for academic performance. Lessons are introduced with the reasons for engaging in the learning task—the reasons might be learning to think critically or exploring the nature of an interesting topic. Students are encouraged to assume responsibility for learning and evaluating their own work and the work of others. Interaction may include a discussion of the validity of explanations, the search for more information, the testing of various explanations, or consideration of the pros and cons of specific decisions.

The characteristics that distinguish new collaborative approaches to math and science revolve around group goals and the accompanying benefits of active group work. Instead of being told they need information, students learn to recognize when additional data are needed. They jointly seek it out, apply it, and see its power and value. In this way the actual *use* of science and mathematics information becomes the starting point rather than just an add-on. The teacher facilitates the process, instead of acting as a knowledge dispenser. Student success is measured on performance, work samples, application, or synthesis. Simple recall is not the central feature.

Common themes of a cooperative science and mathematics learning model include an emphasis on exploring a problem, thinking, and the collaborative challenge of posing a solution. This involves peer helping, self-evaluation, and group support for risk taking. It also means accepting individual differences and having positive expectations for everyone in the group. Students understand the purpose of the group task contributes to their own learning and self-development. When the teacher helps children put these elements together, the result is greater persistence and more self-directed learning. To reach such goals also requires viewing classrooms as learning places where teaching methods build on cognitive perspectives rather than coercion.

Getting Started with Collaborative Math and Science Lessons

Getting started with cooperative learning in math and science means defining student and teacher responsibilities. Changing the classroom organization frequently requires change in the physical structure. Mixed ability learning groups of four students have proven effective in mathematics and science classes (Burns, 1977). This may mean adding work tables or pushing chairs together to form comfortable work spaces that are conducive to open communication. It is important to involve students in establishing rules for active group work. Rules should be kept simple and might include the following:

- everyone is responsible for his or her own work
- each person is responsible for his or her own behavior

- everyone must be willing to help anyone who asks
- ask the teacher for help when no one in the group can answer the question.

Group roles and individual responsibilities also need to be clearly defined, and students are usually required to take responsibility for assembling and storing any materials that may be needed.

Teachers need to provide time in their lessons for students to grapple with problems, try out strategies, discuss, experiment, explore, and evaluate. Because the primary focus is on the students' own investigations, discussions, and group projects, the teacher's role shifts to that of an expert manager. By modeling attitudes and presenting themselves as problem solvers and models of inquiry, teachers really become part of the learning process. This makes it clear that everyone is an active scholar and no one knows all the answers. Teachers also need to exhibit an interest in finding solutions to problems, showing confidence in trying various strategies, and risking mistakes. It is more important to emphasize the aspect of *working on the problem* rather than getting "the right answer."

Managing the Cooperative Classroom

To be most effective, teaching must respond to students' prior knowledge and ideas. Therefore, teachers need to *listen* as much as they speak— resisting the temptation to control classroom ideas so that students can get some sense of ownership over their own learning. In a cooperative classroom a give-and-take exists that involves everyone in an open discussion and honest criticism of ideas.

Studies of exemplary teachers reveal strategies which facilitated sustained student engagement. *Controlling at a distance* is one of the most important. This means moving around the room and speaking with individuals and groups from time to time (Tobin & Graser, 1989). Students were able to work independently and cooperatively in groups as they developed a surprising degree of autonomy and independence.

In classrooms identified as "exemplary," students demonstrated the capacity to work together when problems arose, and they knew when to seek help from a peer or the teacher. Teachers were not always worried about maintaining order, nor were they rushing from one student to another (on demand) as hands went up. These teachers had considered all the possibilities and even had time to reflect on the lesson as it progressed. The key to successful monitoring was establishing routines that enabled the teachers to cope with a number of diverse learning needs. In all cases an active student role was emphasized and activities were prescribed to ensure that students were active mentally. And when difficulties were encountered, students were encouraged to try to work them out for themselves, to consult resources and peers (Shulman & Colbert, 1987).

Many exemplary teachers also tended to explain task requirements. When off-task behavior occurred, the teachers quickly and quietly spoke to the individual, pairs, or small groups concerned. They did so in a manner that did not disrupt the work of students who were on task. Model teachers also used strategies which encouraged students to actively participate in learning activities. They allowed students to participate without embarrassment, which proved particularly beneficial for relatively quiet students. These excellent teachers were also good at connecting learning with thinking and understanding most frequently through the use of concrete materials.

By encouraging verbal interactions among groups, the teacher can learn to monitor students' understanding of the content and occasionally ask questions to stimulate thinking. By probing students' responses, teachers in a cooperative learning environment can get students to elaborate and clarify their thinking and speculations. Teachers can provide examples and additional information to groups when they are stuck (Meyer & Sallee, 1983). The research suggests that the most successful problem-solving approaches involved direct materials-centered experiences and peer assistance in developing critical thinking and interpersonal skills. Finally, exemplary teachers used the features of a quality math and science program to maintain an environment where students viewed mathematics and science in a favorable light (Clark, Carter, & Sternberg, 1988).

Strategies for Teaching the Cooperative Group Lesson

When teaching a lesson, it is important that students understand the problem situation and work together to find and evaluate the solution. Specific strategies that have proven helpful:

Introduce the Lesson. During the initial introduction the teacher's objective is for the students to understand the problem or skill and establish guidelines for the group's work. The teacher presents or reviews the necessary concepts or skills with the whole class and poses a part of the problem or an example of a problem for the class to try. Opportunities for discussion are provided. The actual group problem is then presented after the conceptual overview. The class is encouraged to discuss and clarify the problem task. Before breaking the class into groups, it is helpful to have a student or two explain the problem back to the class in their own words. This summary of the teacher's directions can help clarify, define, and set up the group task. This also helps the teacher promote thinking skills and insure an understanding of the problem task. Students then break into small learning groups as assigned.

Time for Groups To Explore. Students work cooperatively to solve the problem. The teacher observes, listens to the groups' ideas, and offers assistance as needed. The teacher is also responsible for providing extension activities when a group is done early. If a group is having difficulties, the teacher helps them discover what they know so far, poses a simple example, or perhaps points out a misconception or erroneous idea of the group. Sometimes a group has trouble getting along or focusing on what they are supposed to be doing. At this time it may be necessary to refocus the group's attention by asking questions such as: What are you supposed to be doing? What is the task? How will you get organized? What materials do you need? Who will do what?

Summarize. After the problem task and group exploration are completed, students again meet as a whole class to summarize and present their findings. Groups present their solutions and share their processes. When the processes are shared, both group procedures and problem solving strategies are summarized.

Questions might include: How did you organize the task? What problems did you have? What method did you use? Was your group method effective? Did anyone have a different method or strategy for solving the problem? Do you think your solution makes sense? Encourage students to generalize from their results. What other problem does this remind you of? What other follow-up experiment could you try, based on your findings? Students are encouraged to listen to and respond to other students comments. It may also be helpful to make notes of the responses on the chalkboard to help summarize the class data at the close of the lesson.

A Sample Cooperative Activity

Cooperative group learning in math and science allows students to participate in activities that serve as a basis for observation as well as reflection. Math and science activities frequently center around general principles relating to the topic being studied. Students are asked to explore problems and form generalizations that direct their applications in new situations (Chickering, 1977). The pooling of tasks, exercises, and games involves students directly in cooperative interactions with their peers. Cooperative experiential learning activities involve concrete experiences, observation, making generalizations, reflection, the forming of concepts, and testing or applying concepts to new situations.

Concrete Experiences. In this beginning group activity, students are asked to survey the group and prepare a group poster or graph that reflects the ideas of every member of the class. This exposes the group to a range of cooperative procedures. The group must exchange ideas (What do we want to find out? What will it look like? What topic should we choose?) and share feelings (What are we going to do? How do we organize it?). Lack of specific instructions can lead to frustration in some individuals. Members must help each other organize, plan, and produce a product. Each group presents their work to the class and reports on how their group arrived at the finished product. Hanging the graphs on posters creates a sense of belonging as a group.

Observation and Reflection. Learners reflect on the experience's significance for them. This is a bridge between the experience and formal learning role as observers. Students are asked to examine these questions:

- *What happened in your group?* Students share perceptions with each other. This allows them to recognize that not all members perceive the event the same.
- *How did the group participants feel?* (Positive, negative, trust, and acceptance factors are revealed, as well as elements of "risk" and exposure.
- *What does it mean?* Students explore meaning, generalize, and examine group roles.

Formalization of Abstract Concepts and Generalizations. To help students interpret the knowledge gained through the experience and as a guide to application, teachers may wish to assign follow-up readings, activities, or assignments that involve the use of surveys, graphing, or data presentation.

Testing Applications in New Situations. Based on what they found out, students may wish to choose a new topic to study or create new group tasks with a real-world emphasis. The more complex the thinking and the higher-order processing of information, the greater the effect on problem-solving social skills and attitudes.

ACTIVE LEARNING ACTIVITIES
NUMERACY, MATHEMATICS, AND SCIENCE

Learning is enhanced by presenting information in multiple formats, including multisensory activities and experimental opportunities. Some of these include concrete manipulatives like geopieces, cuisinaire rods, blocks, fraction pieces, base ten blocks, popsicle sticks, chips, and so on. Other activities include TV programs, computer simulations, role-playing problems, and instructional courseware. These cooperative group activities have proved highly motivational and effective at reaching multiple learning styles.

1. *Math/Science Nature Search* (elementary)

 Mathematics and science application a re all around us. Mathematical patterns in nature abound. Architecture, art, and everyday objects rely heavily on mathematical principles, patterns, and symmetrical geometric form. Students need to see and apply real world connections to concepts in science and mathematics. This activity is designed to get students involved and more aware of the mathematical/scientific relationships around them and to use technology to help report their findings.

 Divide the class into four groups. Each group is directed to find and bring back as many objects as they can that meet the requirements on their list. Some objects may need to be sketched out on paper if they are too difficult to bring back to the classroom, but encourage them to try to bring back as many as possible.

 • *Group One: Measurement Search*

 Find and bring back objects that are:

   – as wide as your hand   – a foot long
   – further away than you can throw   – waist high
   – half the size of a baseball   – as long as your arm
   – smaller than your little finger   – wider than four people
   – thinner than a shoelace   – as wide as your nose.

 • *Group Two: Shape Search*

 Find and bring back as many objects as you can that have these shapes:

 -triangle   circle   -square   -diamond
 -oval   -rectangle   -hexagon   -other geometric shapes

 • *Group Three: Number Patter Search*

 Find objects that show number patterns. For example, a three-leaf clover matches the number pattern three.

 • *Group Four: Texture Search*

 Find as many object as you can that have the following characteristics:

 -smooth   -rough   -soft   -grooved/ridges -hard
 -bumpy   -furry   -sharp   -wet   grainy

 When students return, have them arrange their objects in some type of order or classification. Using a graphing program on the computer or colored paper, scissors and markers, have them visually represent their results in some way (bar graph, for example).

2. *Student-Generated Problems*

   Have student groups construct their own problems on a topic of their choice. Encourage them to use survey data, newspaper stories, or current information from education television. Encourage calculator use.

3. *Data Surveys & Graphing*

   Divide the class into small groups of four or five. Have them brainstorm about what they would like to find out form the other class members (favorite hobbies, TV shows, kinds of pets, etc.). Once a topic is agreed upon and OK'd by the teacher, have them organize and take a survey of all of the class members. Remember, several groups will be doing this at once, so allow some noise and movement.

   When the statistics are gathered and compiled, each group must make a clear descriptive graph which can be posted in the classroom. Encourage originality and creativity.

4. *World Population Statistics* (middle school)

   Charts and graphs are visual communication forms that reveal statistical data at a glance. These visual models can help lead to a better understanding of global problems and real-world situations. Using world population statistics and calculators, have student groups made comparisons between land size and population. Some sample activities:
   - Graph the regions by size according to population, and land size.
   - Calculate how many people per square kilometer in each continent. Chart your answer.
   - Describe what you can infer about each continent by looking at these statistics.
   - Look up annual food production for a region of your choice. Write a description of how this compares to its land size and population.

5. *Collecting & Analyzing TV Data*

   Have students survey their families viewing habits. The survey questions could follow the same format as the Nielson survey data. This kind of survey includes what programs are watched, what time the TV is on, how many people are watching at a time, and so on. Compose the survey instrument with the class based on information they would like to find out. (A note to parents outlining the intent of the activity and the assignment is helpful.) After the students have gathered the data for a week's time, have them summarize the information in their group. Compare such items as the average time spent watching TV for the group, most popular times for watching, most popular shows, and so on. These are excellent ways to integrate charts and graphs into social education and values clarification activities. Questions such as How much TV viewing is good? What other things do you give up when you spent time watching television? How much talking goes on while the TV set is on? can be explored.

Ask for volunteers to spent 1 week not watching television. This group should keep a record of what they did instead of watch television. Encourage volunteers to share their reactions to the experiment with the class.

6. *Mathematics and Science In the World of Work*
Have students gather information a bout mathematics and science in the workplace and careers that spark their interest. Draw up a simple survey form listing occupations that students are interested in, and spaces to gather data about ways mathematics and science is used on the job. Have student groups interview workers, parents, community professionals, and friends to find out how they use science and mathematics tools in their work.

Have groups assemble and display the data in visual form (charts, graphs, etc.) Look for patterns and comparisons. Are there generalizations that can be made? Conclusions that can be drawn?

7. *Using Community Resource*
Museums are one way to link science and community resources. Students can play the role of curators. Working in pairs have students investigate objects such as bones, fossils, shells, and so on. Have students find out all they can about the object using the full range of resources available at the museum or naturalist center.

To add an element of interest and adventure, have student in groups of four crate a fictitious but plausible scenario to accompany an object of their choice. In one story students were told the bone was brought to them by the FBI, which expressed concern that it might be human. (The Smithsonian actually gets may such cases each year.) Student groups must try to determine the origin; if not a human bone, then they are to find what animal the bone belonged to, what part of the skeleton, etc. At the end of the activity student groups to the class and present their problem and the findings.

8. *Cooperative Construction: Building Bridges*
This is an interdisciplinary activity which reinforces skills of communication, group process, social studies, language arts, mathematics, science, and technology.

Materials:
Lots of newspaper and masking tape, one large, heavy rock, and one cardboard box. Have students bring in stacks of newspaper. you need approximately one foot of newspaper per person. Bridges are a tribute to technological efforts which employ community planning, engineering efficiency, mathematical precision, aesthetics, group effort, and construction expertise.

Procedures:
a. For the first part of this activity, divide students into three groups.

Each group will be responsible for investigating one aspect of bridge building.

Group One: Research
This group is responsible for going to the library and looking up facts about bridges, collecting pictures of kinds of bridges, and bringing back information to be shared with the class.

Group Two: Aesthetics, Art, Literature
This group must discover songs, books, about bridges, paintings, artwork, etc, that deal with bridges.

Group Three: Measurement, Engineering
This group must discover design techniques, blueprints, angles, and measurements of actual bridge designs. If possible, visit a local bridge to look at the structural design, and so on. Each group presents its findings to the class. The second part of this activity involves actual bridge construction by the students.

b.   Assemble the collected stacks of newspaper, tape, the rock, and the box at the front of the room. Divide the class into groups of four or five students. Each group is instructed to take an even portion of newspaper and one or two rolls of masking tape. Explain that the group will be responsible for building a stand–alone bridge using only the newspapers and tape. The bridge is to be constructed so that it will support the large rock and so that the box can pass underneath.

c.   Each group is give 3 to 5 minutes of planning time in which they are allowed to talk and plan together. During the planning time they are not allowed to touch the newspapers and tape,but they are encouraged to pick up the rock and make estimates of how high the box is.

d.   At the end of the planning time students are given 10 to 12 minutes to build their bridge. During this time there is no talking among the group members. They may not handle the rock or the box, only the newspapers and tape. (A few more minutes may be necessary to ensure that all groups have a chance of finishing their constructions.)

Evaluation:
Stop all groups after the allotted time. Survey the bridges with the class and allow each group to try to pass the two tests for its bridge. (Does the bridge support the rock, and does the box fit underneath?) Discuss the design of each bridges and how it compared to the bridges researched earlier.

Follow-up/Enrichment:
As a follow up activity,have each group measure its bridge and design a

blueprint (includes angles, length, and width of the bridge) sot hat another group could build the bridge by following this model.

9. *Concept Circles and Venn Diagrams*

Science teachers can make use of a variety of diagrams to help students grasp important concepts. Like mapping, concept circles demonstrate meaning and develop visual thinking. Have student groups represent their understanding of science concepts by constructing concept circles following these rules:

- Let a circle represent any concept (plant, weather bird...)
- Print the name of that concept inside the circle.
- When you want to show that one concept is included within another concept draw a smaller circle within a larger circle, for example, large circle planets, smaller circle earth.
- To demonstrate that some elements of one concept are part of another concept, draw partially overlapping circles. Label each (water contains some minerals). The relative size of the circles can show the level of specificity for each concept. Bigger circles can be used for more general concepts, or used to represent relative amounts.
- To show two concepts are not related, draw two separate non connected circles and label each one (bryophytes—mosses, without true leaves; tracheophytes—vascular plants with leaves, stems, and roots)

10. *Active Research: Exploring Pollution in the Earth Spheres*

Pollution is defined as an undesirable change in the properties of the lithosphere, hydrosphere, atmosphere, or ecosphere that can have deleterious effects on human and other organisms. Apart of the task for student teams is to decide what an undesirable change is, or what is undesirable to them.

Tell the teams they care going to classify pollution in their neighborhood and city. The classification will be based on their senses and the different spheres of the earth: lithosphere (earth's crust), hydrosphere (earth's water), atmosphere (earth's gas), and ecosphere (the spheres in which life is formed). Give each group an observation sheet or have it design one that shows examples of pollution for a week.

OBSERVATIONS OF POLLUTION AND EARTH SPHERES

SENSES	LITHOSPHERE	HYDROSPHERE	ATMOSPHERE	ECO-SPHERE
sight				
touch				
hearing				

taste

smell

Student teams are to record the types of pollution observed in the different earth's spheres. After a week of data gathering, discuss the groups' observations with the class. Teams may not have completed all the boxes of information. Discuss why they occurred. Also discuss discrepancies in groups' data and the reasons for this. Ask the class to identify the source of pollution and predict what might happen if the pollution continued.

Have the groups figure out visual presentations of their data (slides, video, charts, graphs, newspaper story and illustrations, etc.). Class projects like these are frequently of interest to community organization and news media.

11. *Using Video Segments To Teach*

Tape short segments from televisions science and technology programs which deal with issues and concepts in your curriculum. Excerpts from science programs like "NOVA," "Wild Kingdom," "Science and Technology Week," "3-2-1 Contact," or even the Weather Channel and the evening news offer a wealth of material. Design short projects based on these segments: an endangered species mural, a chart of weather patterns for the country, a computer newsletter, an audio taped radio news release, and so on. Student teams are great at coming up with their own projects, especially once you've sparked their interest on a topic.

12. *Newspaper Science and Mathematics*

Major newspapers like the *New York Times* and the *Washington Post,* or the daily paper in local areas, frequently have weekly science and technology sections. Select a list of significant terms from the lead stories, pass out the papers or photocopies of the articles, and have students construct science stories with the words and ideas from the feature science news paper.

13. *Calculator Activities To Promote Numeracy*

How much is a billion? How long would it take to count up to a billion, if you counted one number per second? Take a guess. Write it down. Use a calculator to find out. The result may surprise you.

- *Counting with a calculator:* The calculator can be used as a powerful counting tool. Important concepts of sequencing, place value, and one-to-one correspondence are learned through a child's physical interaction with this almost magical counting device.

  To make a calculator count: enter the number 1 and press the + sign. Press the + sign again. Next press the = sign. Continue to press =. The calculator will begin counting. Each time the = sign is pressed, the next number in sequence appears on the screen. If this set of instructions doesn't work with your calculator, check its directions. The directions should indicate how to get a constant function. Follow the directions on how to get a constant and any of the countering activities will work for you.

- *Counting backwards:* A calculator can also be programmed to count backwards. Start with the number 1. Next push the − sign. Push the − sign again, and then the number you want to count backwards from. For example, if you wanted to count backwards from 100, enter $1 - 100 = = =$. When you press $=$ the calculator should show 99. Continue to press $=$. With each press of the $=$ button the next number in reverse sequence appears. This is a great way to introduce children to counting backward.

- *Skip Counting:* A calculator can skip count also Encourage students to count by 100s and 1000s. Or try skip counting by 3s, 5s, 7s, 9s, or whatever. You can begin counting with any number and skip count by any number. Have students try these calculator-counting exercises, then make up their own. Encourage speculation about what the next number will be. Can find a pattern?

  $5 + + 10 = = = =$

  $3 + + = = =$

  $100 - - = 1000 = = =$

  Try having a counting race. How long does it take counting by 1s to count to 1000. How long would it take counting by 100s to count to 1,000,000?

14. *Creative Visualization: Rock Guided-Imagery Experience*

    Guided imagery is much like a story. The teachers guides students through an imaginary journey, encouraging them to create images or mental pictures and ideas. This activity should be done in a quiet relaxed atmosphere. Teachers may wish to dim the lights or have student rest at their desks while they read the visualization. After reading have student follow up with some kind of creative activity: discussing their experience in their group, writing in their science log, or creating an artistic expression of some kind.

A Rock

Close your eyes and imagine that you are walking in a lush green forest along a trail. As you are walking you notice a rock along the trail. Pick up the rock. Now make yourself very, very tiny, so tiny that you become smaller than the rock. Imagine yourself crawling around on the rock. Use your hands and feet to hold onto the rock as you scale up its surface. Feel the rock. Is it rough or smooth? Can you climb it easily? Put your face down on the rock. What do you feel? Smell the rock. What does it smell like? Look around. What does the rock look like? What colors do you see? Is there anything unusual about your rock? Lie on your back on the rock and look at the sky. How do you fee? Talk to the rock. Ask it how it got there, ask how it fees to be a rock. What kind of problems does it have? Is there anything else you want to ask the rock or talk to the rock about? Take a few minutes to talk to the rock and listen to its answers. When you're done talking, thank the rock for allowing you to climb and rest on it. Then carefully climb down off the rock. When you reach the ground gradually make yourself larger until you are yourself again. When you are ready, come back to the classroom, open your eyes and share your experience.

15.   *Using Logo Programming with Young Learners*
Seymour Papert developed the Logo language to teach geometric concepts. He believes students can learn mathematical relationships more efficiently if they can project themselves into the world of mathematics. Students who can program a computer to draw a square or circle must understand the nature of a square or circle well enough to "teach" the computer. Using a logo program such as LogoWriter, even young student teams can develop short procedures and program the computer. Here are a few sample procedures using Logo Writer.

To Yellow Square
sect 4
repeat 4[fd 40 rt 90]
end
    To red rectangle:
setc 3
repeat 2[fd 40 rt 90 fd 80 rt 90]
Wait 60 cg
end

Young students simply type in the words *yellow square* or *red triangle,* and the program will draw what is typed. This is a great way for very young learners to learn colors and shapes and practice reading and spelling thee basic words. Teachers can also program more complicated sentences, add stamped shapes to the program, and make the shapes move across the screen on a typed command from the student. For example, when the student types *A blue rabbit can run,* the program shows the blue rabbit running across the screen. It's really only limited to the teacher's imagination and time constraints.

Combining Subject Matter and the Knowledge of Effective Instruction

In mathematics and science teaching both pedagogical and content area knowledge are important. Without the essential content base teachers will find it difficult to discuss the content or focus students' thinking, and they will have trouble providing appropriate feedback. But people who are just well prepared in mathematics and science will make predictable mistakes (Shulman & Colbert, 1987). Without a knowledge of pedagogy it is difficult to manage a class or make mathematics and science interesting for students.

Traditionally there has been a gap between what was taught in science and mathematics and what was really learned. Interpreting and understanding the real world—and how it relates to personal experience—is different from the interpretations and understandings advanced in school science and math courses. Typical school programs have produced students with increasingly negative attitudes about science and mathematics as they progress through the grades. This is especially true when math and science courses do not consider needs, interests, motivations, or experiences of the learners, or when the material being covered is not viewed as useful or valuable.

In teaching children to think scientifically and mathematically, it is important to help them to apply their understanding and skills in solving problems, discovering relationships analyzing patterns, generalizing relationships, and using numbers with confidence. Incorporating application with collaborative strategies can assist students in taking responsibility for their thoughts as they use higher-level thinking skills and build inner confidence. Scientific literacy will be enhanced over the long haul if programs are developed in an environment that emphasizes cooperative learning.

These new teaching models require combining a cognitive approach with metacognition—thinking about thinking. Students need to think skillfully, and they need to be able to monitor their thinking processes as they work. Constructing a hypothesis, problem solving, critical thinking, and cooperative group work can replace tradition chalk, talk, and textbook methodology. Connecting science and mathematics to each learner's reality and paying attention to interpersonal learning relationships will also help. When these elements are in place science and mathematics *can* be used to solve interesting problems in unique ways.

Recently, technological innovations like calculators and computers have changed the way science and math are taught and learned. New models of instruction that encourage using technology and collaboration have sprung up to deal with this new reality. We are now at a stage where teachers and students must move from seeing technology as a source of knowledge (coach, drill) to viewing it as a medium or forum for communication and intelligent adventure. Making intelligent use of technological innovations requires more thinking, problem formulating, and interpersonal communication skills (Forman & Pufall, 1988).

A substantive knowledge base now exists regarding the social and psychological characteristics of how children learn about mathematics, science, and technology. Yet studies indicate that even experienced teachers are not familiar with this knowledge (Carey, Mittman, & Darling-Hamand, 1989). The challenge is to make research-based knowledge accessible to both practicing teachers and college students in teacher education programs.

Towards A Connected Curriculum

We are just beginning to examine some of the factors that shape mathematical behavior. It's becoming increasingly clear that being able to think scientifically and mathematically requires more than large amount of exposure to content. Students need direct decision-making experiences so that their minds can be broadened by applying science and mathematics. By actively examining and solving problems students can become flexible and resourceful, as they use their knowledge efficiently and come to understand the rules which underlie their domains of knowledge (Hendricksen & Morgan, 1990).

Math researchers examined traditional programs and found that students' foundations (cognitive resources) for problems solving far weaker than their performance on tests would indicate. These studies suggest that even mathematically talented high school and college students (who experienced success in upper division math courses) had little or no awareness of how to use math heuristics (rules of thumb). When faced with nonstandard problems which were not put in a textbook context (oriented toward solutions) students experienced failures and ended up doing distracting calculations and trivia instead of applying the basic concepts at their disposal (Shoenfeld, 1985). Even students who receive good grades in memory-based programs frequently have serious misconceptions about mathematics, science, and their relationship to real life activities. Implementing well-learned mechanical procedures in domains where little is understood is one thing— deep learning and application is quite another.

Heroic efforts and a change in thinking will be needed if we are going to create a workforce that is scientifically literate and numerate. Science and math skills taught in isolation lead to isolated thinking and infrequent use in real world situations. There is a need for science and mathematics to be integrated with language arts, visual and performing arts, social studies, movement, and technology. Understanding the need for all children to talk, think, and act scientifically is equally important if we are to enter a more mature period in human history.

One of the most important conclusions of the current research on higher order thinking skills is that transfer of skills from one area to another does not occur automatically. Some students intuitively see connections between mathematics, science, critical thinking, and problem solving—others do not. For many, generalizations must be planned or they may not occur. The research suggests that, if teachers are aware of and actively promote generalizations, transfer to real-world situations will be more likely (Clewell, 1987).

Learning moves along a path from concrete experiences to abstract manipulations. An important instructional principle, strongly validated by recent educational research, is that children learn science and mathematics more effectively when they can concretely connect experiences with the principles they are studying in various subjects (Langbort & Thompson, 1985). Developing an understanding of the complexity of real-world issues means examining multiple perspectives.

The success factor is strongly related to the amount of learning that takes place in studying math and science. Even if students are actively engaged, they learn most effectively only when the are performing mental activities with reasonable rates of success. In math and science classroom students' efficiency of learning is also related to the extent that their class and study time is turned into academic learning time. This means that the longer students actively attend to a task, the higher the rate of success (Stenmark, Thompson, & Cossey, 1986). With numeracy and scientific literacy comes confidence that relates to other subjects and real-life situations..

The Future of Scientific Literacy

> *The years doors open like those of language to the unknown.*
> *Last night you told me we shall have to think up signs,*
> *Sketch a landscape,*
> *Fabricate a plan on the double page of day and paper.*
> *Tomorrow, we shall have to invent once again the reality of this world.*

> —Elizabeth Bishop

Major steps are required to ensure the goals of scientific literacy are implemented. Among the most significant are:

1. *Improving the teaching of science mathematics and technology*
   Effective teaching must be based on learning principles of research and practice. These include providing students with active hands-on experience, placing emphasis on students' curiosity and creativity and frequently using a student team approach to learning. Classrooms should be organized so that small mixed-ability groups are a forum for math/science discussions, discovery, creativity, and connections to other subjects. When students resourcefully collaborate, ask questions, and explore possible answers, they can develop an energetic enthusiasm about these subject. As mathematics and science move from their computational and factual base to a problem-solving emphasis, these subjects can come alive and stimulate students because of their immediacy.

2. *Developing new curriculum models*

   To achieve the goals of scientific literacy, the curricula must be changed to reduce the amount of material covered, to open to cooperative learning practices, and to pay more attention to the collaborative links between mathematics, science, and technology. The scientific endeavor must be presented as a social phenomenon that influences human thought and action.

3. *Initiating collaborative partnerships on many levels*

   To succeed, reform must be collaborative involving teachers, administrators, university faculty, and representatives from business, labor, government agencies and the community.

Tomorrow will bring different solutions to the best that we can envision today. Consequently, innovation and planning must occur without too many preconceived notions. Once programs are in place, new pictures emerge and programs will have to change with changing social and individual needs. Whatever new realities fall into place to change our views, there is no reason why scientific literacy cannot be achieved by all students in the United States. It's a matter of national commitment, determination, and a willingness to collaborate toward common goals.

REFERENCES

Americans Association for the Advancement of Science. (1990). *Science for all Americans*. Washington, D.C. Author

Aronowitz, S.D. (1990). *Science as power: Discourse and ideology in modern society.* Minneapolis, MN: University of Minnesota Press.

Bruner, J., & Haste, H. (1987). *Making sense.* New York: Routledge.

Burns, M. (1977). *The good times math event book.* Oak Lawn, IL: Creative Publications.

Carey, N., Mittman, B., & Darling-Hammand, L. (1989). *Recruiting mathematics and science teachers through nontraditional programs: A survey.* Santa Monica, CA: Rand Corporation.

Champagne, A., & Klopfer, L. (1988). Research in science education: The cognitive perspective. *Research within reach: Science education.* Washington, DC: American Association for the Advancement of Science.

Chickering, A. (1977). *Experience and learning.* New Rochelle, NY: Change Magazine Press.

Clark, C., Carter, B., & Sternberg, B. (1988). *Math in stride.* Menlo Park, CA: Addison-Wesley.

Clewell, B.C. (197). What works and why: Research and theoretical bases of intervention programs in math and science for minority and female students. In A.B. Champagne & L. E. Hornig (Eds.), *This year in school science 1987: Students and science learning* (pp. 95-135). Washington, DC: American Association for the Advancement of Science.

Cockroft, W. (1986). *Mathematics counts.* London: Her Majesty's Stationary Office.

Dossey, I., Mullis, M., Linquist, M., & Chambers, D. (1988). *The mathematics report card.* Princeton, NJ: Educational Testing Service.

Forman, G., & Pufall, P. (Eds.). (1988). *Constructivism in the computer age.* Hillsdale, NJ: Erlbaum.

Garofalo, J. (1988). Metacognition and school mathematics. *The Arithmetic Teacher, 34*(3), 22-23.

Hendricksen, B., & Morgan T. (Eds.). (1990). *Reorientations: Critical theories and pedagodies.* Champagne, IL: University of Illinois Press.

Langbort, C., & Thompson, V. (1985). *Building success in math.* Belmont, CA: Wadsworth Publishing.

Meyer, C., & Sallee, T. (1983). *Make it simpler: A practical guide to problem solving in mathematics.* Menlo Park, CA: Addison-Wesley.

Miller, J. (1990). [Survey data from Northern Illinois University's Public Option Laboratory.]

National Assessment of Educational Progress. (1989). Washington, DC: U.S. Government Printing Office.

National Council of Teachers of Mathematics. (1989). *Curriculum & evaluation standards for school mathematics.* Reston, VA: Author.

Paul, R., Binker, K., Jensen, K., & Kreklau,H. (1989). *Critical thinking handbook.* Rohnert Park, CA: Sonoma State University.

Paulos, J. (1988). *Innumeracy.* New York: Hill and Wang.

Peterson, P.L. (1988). Teachers' and students' cognitional knowledge for classroom teacher and learning. *Educational Research, 17*(5), 5-14.

Shoenfeld, A. (1985). *Mathematical problem solving.* Orlando, FL: Academic Press.

Shulman, J. (1986). Paradigms and research programs in the study of teaching: A contemporary perspective. In M. Wittrock (Ed.), *Handbook of research on teaching* (3rd, pp. 3-36). New York: Macmillan.

Slavin, R. (1989). *School and classroom organization.* Hillsdale, NJ: Erlbaum.

Steen, L. A. (1990). Numeracy. *Daedalus, 119*(2), 211-231.

Stenmark, J., Thompson, V. R., & Cossey, R. (1986). *Family math.* Palo Alto, CA: Dale Seymour Press.

Tobin, K., & Graser, B. (1989). Case studies of exemplary science and mathematics teaching. *School Science and Mathematics, 89*(4), 17-24

5

EDUCATIONAL COMPUTING & COLLABORATION

The Multimedia Computer Platforms of the 1990s— and Making Good Use of School Computers from the 1980s

Chance favors the prepared mind.
—Louis Pasteur

Literacy, numeracy, creative thinking, being able to work in groups, and understanding the communications media of the time are at or near the top of everyone's educational priority list. Computers from the early 1980s caused spontaneous talk about problem solving, writing, and graphics as children and teachers passed by the screen or waited for turns (Silvern, 1988). Today the intersection of computers, video, sound, and animation is adding a new dimension to computing. Advancing technology, like multimedia computing, can have a liberating effect on the imagination—and the school budget.

Multimedia adds a fresh perspective to educational computing. This communications technology can have a positive effect on creative work that goes beyond the simple influence to forcing communicators out of established patterns and into new learning worlds of real and artificial collaboration. When the excitement of discovery is assisted by peers and the imaginative spirit of inquiry, learning is at its best.

When technological and human horizons are in the process of changing, a sort of flexible drive and intent are required for innovation and progress. Technology adds power to the situation. Computers and their media associates can help us kick against educational boundaries and expand horizons. Using computer platforms with new multimedia possibilities allows learners to browse more effectively between subjects, reading something here, and viewing a video segment there.

The vivid images of multimedia computing enable users to move quickly through mountains of information, pulling out concepts that are interesting to the user. By breaking down structural barriers, multimedia changes what we do with computers—and how we view computer-generated information. As routines, organizational, and technological patterns change, some of the basic assumptions about learning will need to be rethought.

Changing Perspective

Alexander Graham Bell thought, when he invented the telephone, that it would quickly be used by every business. It wasn't. But in his wildest imagination he never realized that, in the more distant future, there would be one in every home. Even the best thinkers often *overestimate* technology in the short run—and *underestimate* its long-run potential.

Is there a relationship between luck, preparation, and creative thinking? It's often difficult to detect the subtle happenstance and how we make room in our own lives for positive accidents to happen. A quizzical mind notices and encourages things. Following curiosity and making enough room to encourage luck in any process involves dealing with knowledge.

Amplifying luck—training the eye to notice things—allows you to go a long way towards *making* your own luck. Being exposed to different experiences and paying attention opens up all kinds of possibilities. By amplifying frames of reference, better inferences can be made (as to meaning). Each new finding can lead to fresh questions and changing horizons. This is important, because such a breaking of habits is required for creative thinking.

Anything that changes perspective, from travel to technology to human teaching, can help generate new ideas. Playfulness and experimentation can also open a person up to creative possibilities. These might be described as increasing the capacity to solve problems or fashion products in a novel but ultimately useful fashion. Playing with various ideas may result in getting lucky with one or two of them.

The creative, playful gleam in the eye is an engine of progress. The main reason for learning a lesson is its potential influence on our understanding or behavior, its "instrumental utility." There are multiple tools and modes of expression—and schools must use all of them to promote the multitude of strengths and imaginations found in all students. Curriculum goals are best if they are aimed at the growth of understanding rather than the coverage of state-mandated information.

It is difficult to unravel issues of creativity and what should be learned without taking into account influential communication media. The most competent and experienced eventually learn to sort out the important from the trivial. The yeast of knowledge, openness, and enterprise raises the need for a multiplicity of learning media. We shape our technological tools and they shape us. Some, like *television,* are often written about as Lady Caroline Lamb wrote about Byron: *"mad, bad, and dangerous to know."* The power of short-lived electronic messages is crowding out civic knowledge with MTV-like trivia. As the world is saturated with the best manufactured images, all that's remembered is the sensational and the cute.

Yet TV's vivid images, wide accessibility, and mass appeal are not to be dismissed. And when it's made interactive by a computer platform, users can gain some control while accessing massive amounts of information. The result can foster the kind of visually intensive literacy that is so important in a technological world.

Visual Perception and Multimedia

Combinations of media can best bring out various aspects of a subject and increase students competency with different communications media. To imagine is to generate images. By incorporating visual elements, technology can serve as a stimulant to learning and a forum for dialogue on issues that enhance or challenge the community. One of the major communications technologies being developed for the 1990s is multimedia. Art is as much a part of this as is science. Multimedia provides a smooth ramp for bringing more visual elements into computing. A multimedia toolkit for educators often includes a CD-ROM player (plus speaker for sound), a videodisc player (for moving video access), and a computer (like the Apple Macintosh). This more creative role for the computer is changing the way we think and learn.

Multimedia is more than a trendy buzz word—it makes computers and television equal partners in the creative process. Subjects like literature and art can be participatory and based on collective experience. The program is no longer like a remote conductor directing an orchestra while people sit calmly in their seats. The *doers* don't have to be separated from the *watchers*. They can illustrate pictures, change the musical score, or decide on the direction of the story.

With its own set of values multimedia can form the basis of a collective experience for a small group of learners. It can allow for computer users to delve into their work by creating both elaborate static art and animation. It can also allow for small group experiences with traditional art. Shared art, like shared history, has a legitimate vocabulary. The thoughtful perception generated by art often anticipates change in social structures. In new multimedia designs the visual world is treated as a quantity to be explored. Multimedia allows us to construct images from transactions with art, science, literature, drama, dance, poetry, and music.

Art is often controversial, and what we may treasure today was once considered heretical. It is not meant to be comfortable and soothing. Museums serve as forums open to a wide range of artistic or scholarly works. We now have whole museums on videodiscs and CD-ROMs that can be accessed by new multimedia computers to examine society in all its complexity. Such access can serve to stimulate dialogue on neglected issues and deal with issues from a different perspective. It makes for good art and a good use of technology.

Much of the public will never have an opportunity to see some art if technological access is not allowed. Educators must sometimes accept images that are disconcerting, and schools must protect art just as they protect good literature. If art is not at least occasionally controversial, it will become bland. It's a small step from censoring art to censoring language, literature, and school textbooks. When things are even briefly bothered by small groups with prohibitions in mind, there is a chilling effect on the next decision. The result of pressure tactics by adversity of small groups is that only pablum passes easily.

A democracy's test is to make the arts and humanities accessible to the people. Once you begin to deny technological tools that make for easy access or impose restriction on art, you start to limit options. By removing inhibitions to changing language, for example, we may be able to remove some of the destructive barriers to imaginative usage.

Freedom can be measured as well in what is lost as it can in what has been gained. Positive growth and change is as much a divorce from the past as it is an embrace of the future. With, or without technology, there is no such thing as *complete* freedom. That's a dream in a dreamer's mind; but the more we strive to use our minds and tools intelligently, the closer we will get to it.

Contributing To Educational Improvement

To be valuable, educational technology, like educational research, must contribute to the improvement of education (Mandell & Mandell, 1989). Teachers and their technological tools can help open doors on reality and provide a setting for reflection. Both can make important points that might otherwise go unnoticed. Drawing on the arts and humanities as sources of inspiration while making a continuous case for observation and effective literature is a convincing way to bring the schooling process to life. Two examples available today are The Voyager Company's Beethoven program ("Symphony No. 9") and ABC Interactive's videodisc and Hypercard Stacks ("In the HolyLand").

Progress will be limited if we are forced to use traditional instructional delivery models—ask and tell, tell and ask, technology and students (one on one). New findings in cognitive development, collaborative learning, and communications point to highly interactive active learning models (Ede & Lunsford, 1986). As new technologies and related products bring us closer to maximizing learning, the process of presenting, training, education, and entertainment is bound to go through more change. This will have a major impact on communication and learning as students become active participants in the knowledge construction process.

As these technological tools come together, they will help students learn at their own pace in a variety of disciplines. Viewed as a technological gateway to learning in the 21st century, multimedia applications are already being applied to a diversity of tasks that give us a better chance of developing the intellectual potential of our students. Multimedia computing is bound to have a major effect on how knowledge is constructed, stored, disseminated, and learned. And if our technological tools can help us to create a spirit of inquiry and love of learning, then the benefactor will be our society.

Seven Uses of Multimedia Systems

- *Illustrating Class Presentations*
  — supporting lecture materials and discussions
- *Creating Courseware*
  — using simulation and problem solving techniques
  — distance learning is another possibility
- *Desktop Publishing and Video Editing*
  — by using authoring systems print, computer graphics, and video may be combined
- *Student Study and Review*
  — students who missed classes or need to review a complex concept can draw on a library of visual aids.
  — intelligent (AI) tutors and telecommunications may soon come into play here.
- *Student Projects*
  — students can develop video projects or "papers."
- *Evaluation and Examination*
  — interactive evaluation techniques hold the potential for going beyond static paper and pencil tests.

- *Access to Print and Video Libraries*
  - vast amounts of print, visual, and sound information can be stored— and quickly retrieved.
  - Hypercard-like linking of information allows the user to electronically "walk" between media and subjects.

USING TODAY'S SCHOOL COMPUTERS TO STIMULATE CREATIVE COLLABORATION

A major difference between collaborative learning before the computer and today's situation is that, now, schools have technological tools that can allow for the dynamic exploration through time, space and ideas in an interactive way. They may not be multimedia wonders, but they can do the job. Computers are proliferating in classrooms around the country. In 1983 the U.S. Office of Education's estimate was 250,000 computers in the schools. Today the number is over 3 million—and nearly all of the schools have at least some of them (Young, 1990). The real question is whether computers are being used to amplify instruction in new ways.

In less affluent schools, district computers tend to be used for drill and practice. In wealthy districts they are more frequently used for enrichment and teaching higher-level thinking skills (Cole, Griffin, & the Laboratory of Comparative Human Cognition, 1987). Is this simply reinforcing the educational mistakes of the past? Each medium should be used for what it does best, without reserving the advanced use of computers for boys or more affluent groups. The way we treat our children tells us a lot about the future we envision.

Computers are a potential educational link between schools and the growing number of poor children, minority children, and immigrant children. Yet schools have just begun to respond to the curriculum changes implied by the computer revolution. Curricula, teaching habits, textbooks, and tests are all products of the precomputer age—which makes it difficult to integrate computers into classroom instruction.

Many argue that computers will not be used effectively in elementary and secondary classrooms until they are used in the learning experiences of teachers themselves. Therefore there is increasing pressure to hire teachers who can use the technology effectively. In addition, the National Education Association has called on every school district to provide computers for every teacher by the year 1991.

To teach today's students effectively means moving beyond how to apply a new piece of computer software to redefining classroom organization. Our focus is on using computers for interactive collaboration—connecting peers, the curriculum, and new representations of knowledge. Research on educational computing and collaboration is more than sufficient to justify the use of both to accelerate student thinking and learning (Vedder, 1985).

Using the Unique Interpersonal Character of Computers

Early computer lessons were rigidly programmed electronic workbooks where individuals took their places in front of the screen and quietly pushed buttons on the keyboard. The computer "taught"; the student was supposed to work and listen in quiet isolation. But that part really didn't work out as planned; students clustered together, sought advice from peer experts, and showed off their skill or product. Contrary to early fears, the use of computers tends to increase (rather than decrease) social skills. Unlike written sheets of paper, writing or graphics on a computer screen are looked upon as something public, more like a book or TV program.

The computer is a natural learning vehicle for cooperative group work. The educational computing-skill practice model still exists, but increasingly programs are being enriched by interactivity. Software that builds on the uniqueness of the computer is making its way into classrooms or computer labs. The computer can now be used to collaboratively learn *how* to do a task—or as a tool for actually *doing* it. For example, students can use the computer to learn some elements of music (and math)—and use it to *make* music.

It took Johannes Kepler 4 years to calculate the orbit of Mars—today students can do in about 4 seconds using a microcomputer. Current information technologies have changed how we think and communicate. They have also vastly increased the capacity to know and do things in a more personalized way. There are new programs like *Critical Thinking and The One Computer Classroom* that are designed to help the classroom teacher build thinking skills across the curriculum.

Among the many untapped facets of computer use is the machine's ability to accommodate a wide range of learning styles. While reading directions on the computer screen appeals to a minority of students who operate well with print-and-listening learning styles, the computer also offers a rich array of graphics for those students who are more visual learners. Computers can be harnessed as tools for multiple ways of thinking. Like the pencil, ruler, or compass the computer's power lies in the user's thoughtful use. It's not the knowledge the computer can teach, as much as it is the way students can use them to explore, compose, create, and experiment.

Computers are rapidly becoming part of elementary and secondary education throughout the country. Many schools have five or more computers (Becker, 1986). A nationwide survey the Center for Social Organization of Schools (1986) estimated schools would need one computer for 12 students just to provide 30 minutes of computer time a day to all students.

The current ratio is about 30 to 1. The extent to which computers are actually used varies. Surveys in 1987 found that, while 70% of elementary teachers had access to computers, only 40% frequently used them (Office of Technology Assessment, 1988).

Roughly the same situation holds true today. Computers are now being used to teach and practice academic subject matter which was formerly presented through lecture or printed materials. Simulation, critical thinking, and problem-solving software are used more infrequently (Kloosterman, Ault, & Harty, 1985). Simulation software, for example, provides more than electronic textbooks. Students can replicate science experiments, recreate historical events, or model business activities. Variables can be altered, the program can be stopped at any stage, and parts of experiments can be reexamined or repeated. New programs, like *Geometric Supposer,* have no predetermined instructional agendas and allow students to collaboratively explore through direct observation, measurement, and experimentation (Yerushalmy, Chazau, & Gorden, 1987).

Word-processing programs, and database and spreadsheet systems, have also found practical applications in schools. Some database programs come with templates for specific subjects, such as social studies; spreadsheets are used in teaching mathematics, and graphing programs are used in algebra and geometry; and programs like TK! Solver, Mathematician, and Idea Processor, are finding their way into school use. For younger students the various versions of Logo have proven that they can foster social interaction and foster the principles of cooperative learning (Maddux & Johnson, 1988).

Computers in the Classroom

In the last 5 years we have begun to see educational software which used the computer's unique characteristics to enhance the learning process. Language arts and English teachers began to incorporate word-processing applications, and spelling and style checkers, giving students powerful new tools for interacting with their writing (Franklin, 1987). In the natural and social sciences, simulations have provided students with innovative experiments and surrogate experiences from history. Information can be embedded in visual narratives to create context that gives meaning to dry facts. Applications in biology, chemistry, engineering, ergonomics, physics, psychology, and physiology allow teachers to create simulations which conform to the normal laws of the universe.

The research suggests that students benefit when they are given control over system parameters so they can explore their effects (Center for Social Organization of Schools, 1986). New computer software, such as *Gravity of the Planets,* allows students to discover algebraic rules, making reasonable estimates about weight and forces of gravity. Students concoct their own problems, such as the weight of the class, pooling resources and information. Working in groups, students discuss, plan, and experiment together. In a similar cooperative vein students can explore museums or works of art—calling up visuals and printed text to explain the history and elaborate the conditions under which the work was created. Thinking skills can be developed differently in the fine arts. The experience of art, for example, cannot be reduced to empirically tested concepts like those that dominate science (Gardner & Perkins, 1989). Through the collaborative use of computers, art can emerge as an even more important source of spiritual information.

Computers have been found to increase socialization among students. The curriculum materials that are most effective and most popular are those that provide for social interaction (Pea & Sheingold, 1987). Students can collaborate by working in pairs on even the more traditional programs. And capitalizing on computer-controlled interactive activities can reach small groups of children through many senses.

A New Approach To the Learning Process

The successful use of computers means involving students and educators in the learning process in new ways. As with any medium, the vitality of computer use depends on talented teachers. Professional knowledge about children, learning, curricula, and classroom organization goes hand in hand with the competencies needed to apply courseware sensibly. Helped along with informed adult energy, computers can do more than facilitate the exchange of ideas and improve writing skills (Office of Technology Assessment, 1988). They can help sharpen a student's power to think critically and develop independent judgments.

The teacher has many roles in structuring collaboration on computers. They include:

- assigning students to mixed-ability teams.
- establishing positive interdependence.
- teaching cooperative social skills.
- insuring individual accountability.
- helping groups process information.

The purpose of team assignment is to ensure a heterogeneous mix of student taking into account ability levels, language differences, race, culture, sex, and behavior patterns. If students haven't worked together before, some structured team-building activities will result in fewer problems later on. Peer tutoring can flourish in such a team-centered computer environment.

Promoting feelings that *no one is successful unless everyone is successful* shapes the way students interact with each other. If this objective is not communicated, students may revert back to traditional individualistic roles out of habit. Methods for getting this point across to students include structuring:

- *Goal Interdependence*—stating clearly what each member of the group should know how to do upon completion of the task
- *Task interdependence*—clearly defining the group goal, and what the team should agree on or be able to produce
- *Resource Interdependence*—specifying parameters, materials, the team's task
- *Role Interdependence*—reviewing the individual roles for the group members; keyboarder, checker, reporter, summarizer, encourager, and so on. Set up the expectation that everyone is responsible for explaining how they came up with the answer. Explain the grading procedures, group credit as well as credit for how well each student performs his or her group job.

Teachers are also involved in teaching of social skills and monitoring to make sure that students continue to use the skill. Teachers select the skill roles they want to teach and emphasize the cooperative strategies to be exhibited by all members. Insuring individual accountability involves making sure that each group member participated, that no student dominated the computer activity or hitchhiked on the group's work without giving his or her share.

The most successful teachers employ a mix of activities like individual interviews, work samples, random member questioning, collecting individual papers at random, or asking individuals to explain the group product. In addition to observing and assisting groups, the teacher is also responsible for processing what was learned in the group activity and making sure that teams reflect on what they did and evaluate the team's efforts.

Neither computers or any other technology will solve our serious social and educational problems. But failing to use the medium will leave the schools less able to cope with these difficulties (Costanzo, 1989). Becoming competent and confident users of this technology is important if the schools are to meet the demands of a changing society. It is equally important to understand the social, economic, political, and educational contexts of the technology that shapes our lives. As these "smart machines" enter into grand alliances with other technologies, they will become common adjuncts to the human teacher and peer group.

There is a social context in which students and teachers interact with computers. In the world outside of school, computers are seen as real collaborative tools for real people. A similar view would be appropriate for schools. Teachers may have to make some changes in how they teach, but computers can never serve as electronic teacher replacements. There is no substitute for educational leaders who bring an "informed exuberance" to the learning environment.

Computers are not for dispensing isolated learning, like the teaching machines of yesteryear (Solomon, 1986). They are instruments to meet integrated social and curricular goals. Computer programs can facilitate thought while serving as a unique and useful supplement to paper, pencils and books. They can also be used for peer tutoring, peer criticism, and group work. Working on computers in cooperative pairs is usually better for beginners than working alone. Sharing with peers, in a supportive small group, is just as important when learning with computers as it is with any other medium.

Peer sharing and coaching can add more active elements to a computer program that is not all that engaging. In opening up avenues of communication educators must decide which technology is best for which students and which set of objectives fit the technology. By the time students get to high school they should be able to develop genuine group goals and use computers to access information, process words, create images and solve problems.

SELECTING HARDWARE AND SOFTWARE

IBM, with its new PS/I, Tandy, and Apple are launching new efforts in the school market. Apple is putting forward a new Macintosh (LC) that not only accommodates Hypercard but can run programs developed for the aging inventory of Apple II computers.

IBM is finally seriously approaching the school market again—after its PCjr failure of the mid-1980s. The new IBM machine is a fairly compact plug-in-and-play system that is easy to operate and comes with Microsoft Works, a program that integrates a word processor, spreadsheet, a database manager, and a communications program. It has a built-in modem that automatically connects to "Prodigy," an electronic information service operated by IBM and Sears. The only problem for schools is the fact that the PS/I has no slots for special function cards, which closes schools off from networking possibilities. It does, however, run most of the PC software that works in IBM school machines.

Choosing computer courseware is heavily influenced by content and lesson objectives as well as the abilities and skills of the student groups involved. As teachers look for software that is adaptive to cooperative learning situations, it may be helpful to ask several questions:

1. What skill is the program trying to teach? And is this a skill that fits into my curricular objectives for cooperative learning?

2. Does the computer courseware create high levels of engagement for student groups?
3. What examples does the program use to teach these skills?
4. What kinds of teaching techniques are used in the program?
5. What prerequisite skills do students need to use this piece of software?
6. Where does this piece of software fit into the learning sequence for this topic?
7. What directions or precomputer activities need to be provided to student teams before using the software?
8. What group activities could serve as a follow-up to this software program?
9. How will individual accountability and group performance be evaluated?
10. What other materials would enhance the skills developed by this program?

There are time consuming evaluation issues surrounding the multitude of software programs to be dealt with. Simulation, Logo microworlds, word processing, interactive literature, spreadsheets, database managers, expert (AI) systems, or getting the computer in contact with the outside world (telecommunications) through a modem/software combination all increase the potential for influencing impressionable minds. That is too large a universe for the teacher to figure out alone. Other teachers who use computers are an excellent source of help with what works in the classroom. Students can also take some of the responsibility. This task is more reasonable and the analysis process itself is an excellent learning vehicle.

It's important to consider whether or not a particular piece of software is motivating and easy to integrate into their instructional program. But the bottom line is: *Do the students like it?* Without question, teachers and students are the ones who experience the consequences of making good or bad choices in software selection. And they are the ones who most quickly learn the consequences of poor choices.

Software Evaluation Criteria

Any software program can be adapted for use in a cooperative learning lesson. To get maximum results from the computer, as well as to benefit from the range of skills of the cooperative group, the following criteria may be helpful:

1. Does the software empower the group, making it more productive than it would be without using the program?
2. Is the software adaptable? Can the team add its own problems or alter the sequence of the program?

3. Does the software meet the age, attention span, and interests of your student groups?
4. Does the program develop, supplement, or enhance the curricular skills you're trying to teach?
5. Is the software easy to use for both teacher and student groups? Does the program require adult supervision or instruction?
6. Groups need to actively control what the program does. To what extent does the program all this?
7. Can the courseware be modified to meet group learning needs and adjusted to the varied learning styles of the members?
8. Does the program have animated graphics which enliven the lesson?
9. Does the program meet instructional objectives and is it educationally sound.
10. Does the program involve higher-level thinking and problem solving?

COLLABORATION SOFTWARE: A FEW NEW FAVORITES

Mathematics

*   *Elastic Lines: The electronic Geoboard* (Grades (2-8)
    Sunburst Communications, Apple family

*   *Exploring Measurement, Time and Money* (Grades K-2)
    International Business Machines, IBM PS/2

*   *Graphics Calculator* (Grades 7-12)
    Conduit, Apple II family

*   *Hands-On Math Volume 1* (Grades K-5)
    Ventura Educational Systems, Apple II or GS

*   *IBM Mathematics Exploration Toolkit* (Grades 8-12 and College)
    International Business Machines, IBM PS/2, IBM PC XT, AT

*   *Maestro Numero*
    The Home School, Tandy, IBM PC and compatibles

*   *Numbermazie* (Grades K-6)
    Great Wave Software, Macintosh

*   *Logo Plus* (Grades K and up)
    Terrapin Software Inc., Apple II family

*   *Talking Math and Me* (Grades K-2)
    Davidson and Associates In. Apple IIGS

Language Arts

- *The Boars Explode* (Grades 2-6)
  Pelican Software, Apple II family

- *The Children's Writing and Publishing Center* (Grades 2 and up)
  The Learning Company, Apple II family, IBM PC and compatibles

- *he Creative Writer* (Grades 1-5)
  Silver Burdett and Ginn, Apple II family

- *The Dinosaur Discovery Kit* (Grades K-3)
  First Byte, Tandy 1000, IBM PC and compatibles, Macintosh Plus, Amiga

- *Explore A Classic* (Grades Pre K-3)
  Bradford Publishing Co. Apple, IBM, Tandy 1000

- *The Puzzle Storybook* (Grades K-3)
  First Byte, Tandy 1000,IBM PC and compatibles, Macintosh, Amiga

- *The New Print Shop*
  Broderbund Software, Apple, MS-DOS

- *The Railroad Snoop for Magic Slate II* (Grades 5-7)
  Sunburst Communications, Apple II family

- *Reading Realities* (Grades 8-12 at risk, reading at Grades 2-6)
  Teacher Support Software, IBM PC/2, Tandy 1000

- *The School Speller for Magic Slate*
  Sunburst Communications, Apple II family

- *Success With Literature* (Grades 7-12)
  Scholastic Software, Apple II family, MS-DOS

- *Super Story Tree* (Grades 4-12)
  Scholastic Software Apple II family

- *Write On!* (Grades K-12)
  Humanities Software, Apple II family, IBM Macintosh

Science

- *Animal Trackers* (Grades 4-10)
  Sunburst, Apple II family

- *Audubon Wildlife Adventures: Grizzly Bears* (Grades 4 and up)
  Advanced Ideas, Apple II family, Apple II GS

- *Bio Sci Lessons (Hypercard)* (Grades K-12) (multimedia)
  Bio Sci Lessons (Videodisc) (Grades K-12)
  Videodiscovery, Macintosh

- *Exploring Science: Temperature* (Grades 7-12)
  Sunburst Communications, Apple II family

- *Learn About Animals* (Grades K-2)
  Sunburst Communications, Apple II family

- *LEGO Technic Control Starter Pack* (Grades 3-12)
  LEGO Dacta

- *Milikan Oil Drop* (Grades 10 and up)
  Vernier Software, IBM PC and compatibles, PS/2, Apple II family

- *Playing With Science: Temperature* (Grades K-7)
  Sunburst Communications, Apple II family

- The Presenter (Grades K-12) (multimedia)
  MECC, Apple

- *Science Toolkit Plus* (Grades 4-12)
  Broderbund Software, Apple II family

- *The Voyager Videostack* (Grades 7-12) (multimedia)
  The Voyager Company, Macintosh

- *Voyage of the Mimi Curriculum Package* (Grades 4-8)
  Sunburst, Apple 64K

- *Wood Car Rally*
  Lunar Greenhouse
  Miner's Cover (Grades 3-8)
  Minnesota Educational Computing Corporation, Apple II family

Social Studies

- *Colonial Times Databases* (Grades 2-6)
  Sunburst Communications, apple II family, Commodore 64

- Culture 1.0 (Grades 9-12 and college)
  Cultural Resources Inc., Macintosh, requires hypercard

- *Hidden Agenda* (Grades 8-12)
  Springboard Software, Inc., IBM PC and true compatibles

- *Our Town Databases* (Grades 4-12)
  Sunburst Communications, Apple II family, Commodore 64

- *PC—Globe* + (Grades 5-12)
  PC Globe, Inc. IBM PC and compatibles, PS/2

- *Time Navigator* (Grade 7 to adult)
  MECC, Apple II series

- *Where In Time Is Carmen Sandiego?*(Grades 6 and up)
  Broderbund Software, Inc. IBM PC, Tandy 1000 and compatibles, Apple II

- *World Geography* (Grade 6 and up)
  Minnesota Educational Computing Corporation, Apple II GS

Creative Arts

- *Cartooners* (Grades K-8)
  Electronic Arts, Apple II GS

- *Paintworks Plus* (Grades K-12)
  Activision Presentation Tools, Apple IIGS

- *Superprint II: The Next Generation*
  Scholastic, Apple II and GS, MS-DOS

- *VCR Companion* (Grades 4-12)
  Broderbund Software Inc., Apple II family, IBM PC and compatibles

Tools

- *IBM Linkway*
  International Business Machines, IBM PC, PS/2

- *Microsoft Works 2.0 For the Mac Plus: Class In a Box* (Grades 7-12)
  Class in a Box 7-12; Teaching Tools for Microsoft Works 2.0
  Microsoft Corporation, Macintosh or better

- Primary Editor Plus (Grades 1-8)
  International Business Machines, IBM PS/2 family

- *Right Writer version 3.0* (Grades 9 and up)
  RightSoft Inc., Inc. IBM PC and compatibles, IBM PS/2

- *Showoff* (Grades 6-12)
  Broderbund Software Inc. Apple II GS

- *Slide Shop* (Grades 4-12)
  Scholastic Software, Apple II family, IBM and compatibles

- *Springboard Publisher II for the Mac* (Grades 4-12)
  Springboard Software, Macintosh Plus and above

Telecommunications

- *Apple Global Education Network*
  Apple Computer

- *Compuserve* (online service)
  call 614-457-8600

- *Iris* (telecommunications (Grades K-12)
  MECC, DOS, Apple II family, Macintosh

- *Kids Network* (Grades 4-6)
  National Geographic Society, Apple IIGS

- *Point To Point* (Grades 7-12)
  Beagle Brothers Inc., Apple IIe, IIGS

- *The Weather Machine* (Grades 7-12)
  National Geographic Society, Apple II family.

ACTIVITIES AND STRATEGIES FOR USING COMPUTERS IN THE COOPERATIVE LEARNING CLASSROOM

Group Software Activities

After a group has completed a software assignment, have the team try one of these activities:

- Make up a quiz about the program and give the questions to another group in the class that has used the program.
- Create your own soundtrack for part of the program.
- Make up a student guide for the program. Use your own directions and illustrations.
- Interview other students who have used the program and write down their responses.
- Write a group review of the program for a magazine.

Integration with Other Materials

After having students use a program involving a subject of theme, assign student teams to research the topic by finding books, films, or TV programs around the same issue. Encourage comparisons between both sets of materials. Have students use the simulation program again and offer insights into the lesson based on their findings. If you have the documentation (instructions) that goes along with the program, then you have another whole set of activities. A mathematics program, for example, is much more powerful if you add real math manipulatives for children to work on in pairs or cooperative small groups.

Skills Practice Tournament

This activity is designed to be used with drill-and-practice software, which reinforces concepts taught but not mastered by students. (Practice on multiplication facts, spelling words, etc., falls into this category.) If students are unfamiliar with the software program, demonstrate the program they will be using. Allow time to answer questions, provide practice demonstrations, etc. Once students are familiar with program:

1. Divide the class into learning teams to practice desired concepts. Structure the teams so that students of varying ability levels are on all teams. Instruct students to practice with their team using the drill and practice software program. Allow time for each team to polish its skills and master the concepts.
2. When students feel their teams are ready, split up the teams into two- to three-person tournament tables composed of members of different teams. It's a good idea to select tournament teams whose members are of similar ability levels (for example, students who have performed well on this skill would be grouped together on one tournament table, and students who were having more difficulty would be grouped together on another).
3. Using the same piece of software, team representatives try to win points for their team. Each student from a tournament table might play three or four rounds of a drill-and-practice activity and keep a record of right and wrong answers for each member of the tournament table.
4. After the tournament, the people at each table with the highest scores (greatest number of correct answers) receive six points to take back to their team. Those with the second highest scores receive four points; those with the least highest number receive two points. Winning teams are determined by total team scores.

Strategies For Team Learning

Before having teams start with the software, it is important to plan the lesson; state objectives; select supporting materials, manipulatives, and so on, and set up students for success. Many software programs lend themselves to precomputer lessons, whether solving problems with manipulative materials such as attribute blocks, creating group compositions or graphics, or doing spreadsheet applications. It is helpful for the group to have encountered the concept before beginning the software or computer lesson. It is also useful to demo the program for the group, using a computer overhead projector, stopping to ask questions, give directions, and receive input. This saves teaching time later on.

Many teachers are facing the problem of having only one computer in the classroom. By setting up activities for both on and off, the computer groups rotate materials and computer time. By demonstrating and answering questions with the whole class, additional efficiency is gained when the group encounters the computer task.

What might the computer classroom of the future look like? A classroom with the full range of today's equipment might give us a hint. You might see a group working with ABC Interactive videodisc on the *Civil Rights Achievement.* A second group could be interacting with the Voyagers videodisc *The Louvre,* using a regular classroom computer and videodisc player. A third group would be using a desktop publishing program preparing publications for a school magazine or make-believe newspaper from a particular period in history. A fourth group could be using Tom Snyder Productions *Television* computer simulation to analyze new media. And a fifth group could be using CD-ROM disc and a telecommunications package to gain access to distant databases and students in different towns.

Computers, Creative Thinking, and Basic Skills

The capacity for technological change often precedes our understanding of the impact that change will have. When it comes to collaboratively using computers to build thinking skills and knowledge of different disciplines, change is visible before its implications are comprehended. Basic skills, computing, and critical and creative thinking need each other. Spontaneity and the creative imagination are elements of achievement central to the development of human thinking and freedom. There is no creative thinking or freedom in a solitary vacuum. A person with a creative style of thinking needs to be stimulated by others. Creative abilities, like connecting disparate concepts or giving novel ideas a chance, requires a mix of traits and abilities. And, when teaching thinking is the question, it is always time to begin. Computer-based learning technologies can embody powerful ideas which can be shared across subject areas.

The intellectual tools developed in one area can foster originality and critical thinking in another. Skills can combine with creative factors to generate learning across a wide range of subjects. Skill without imagination is sterile, while imagination without disciplined skill aborts its image. Although basic and imaginative skills may seem antithetical, one without the other is limiting. In reading, you need a few basic subskills to get started—but without the higher-level context of good literature and imaginative thinking, they lead nowhere. The reverse situation is equally dismal—a great imagination can destroy its potential without at least some skills being in place.

No matter how creative a concept, there is an implicit connection to subskills. For either basic or thinking skills to be developed requires that each area support the other. It is fine to challenge the framework of narrowness often associated with "the basics," for without connections to higher levels of thinking they lead nowhere either. The two areas have a curiously symbiotic relationship. A major difficulty which most teachers encounter is getting students to depart from the skills framework in a disciplined and informed fashion. Computer-based technology can be an informed associate in this process.

There is little question that educational computing has a role to play in helping students develop an unconditional positive regard for one another. Computing would seem to be a natural bridge between the old view of "the basics," thinking skills, and breaking through the artificial limits of school-imposed social isolation. Good teachers can make this technology one more tool in the effort to inspire students to approach their education with a sense of responsibility and possibility.

Bringing Imagination and Skill Together

Computers are not good or bad, they are powerful. Like words, paint, or clay the computer can also be used as an expressive medium. Skills and imagination belong together. In mathematics, for example, the act of creating requires a prerequisite skill base of mathematical structure and pattern. Poetry also relies on the writer's mastery of language, form, and meter. The computer is a medium of human expression which can be used as an extension of these skills and creativity. Imagination and the basics, poetry and mathematics, can emerge from the technology together.

The flexibility of computers allows the imagination to select and combine elements on various levels. Mathematical patterns found in nature, like fractiles, can be generated so that visual models are easily manipulated on the computer for creative problem solving. Thus, the computer allows students to learn problem solving and basic skills in a more dynamic manner.

Like composers who create by sitting at the piano and making things up, the computer also permits creative play. This aspect of computers deserves at least equal time with basic skill building. Children using a Logo program, for example, can manipulate complex geometric concepts in math while creating their own visual compositions with musical accompaniment. The editing process allows them to add, delete, and "arrange" to their satisfaction.

Computer-generated visual models—whether basic skills or flights of fancy—can be manipulated with flexibility and creativity. The opportunity is created for moving across media using computer graphics, numbers, words, or music. Children create their own microworlds, imagine, *and* build skills which can be freely explored. The computer provides a language of thinking and a means of expression where permission is granted to be oneself.

The traditional notion of educators is that, if fluency, flexibility, and originality were systematically taught, true creativity would follow. Unfortunately, it isn't that simple. To begin with, teachers have to teach it. Secondly, fluency doesn't count for much if all the ideas generated are simply trivial. And if flexibility clouds issues or discourages group decision making it can impede learning. Even originality, as traditionally defined by educators, might be simply a social accommodation, rather than either intuitive boundary pushing or barrier breaking.

Unfortunately, the most common school practice encourages children to be plodders who see the rules as conduits for action rather than as collaborative springboards for changing realities. Taking risks, dealing with failure, the desire to be surprised, and enjoying ambiguity are all essential elements in creative behavior. All are difficult for teachers to model and for many students to accept. After all, simply accepting the directions from someone in authority is always easier.

In the real world we learn more about creativity from our failures, accidents, and the personal restructuring of our reality in the face of uncertainty. Gaining the help of a supportive group reduces the fear of failure. This fear prevents some students from even trying creative activities. The computer can rekindle interest by allowing the students to take risks and make mistakes without a loss of self-esteem.

As a dynamic communication instrument the computer can act as a generator for collaboration, creativity, and skill building. Students, even if they are great distances apart, can use the computer and a modem to jointly create new ideas and look at basic skills in a new way. Computers can also give visual dimension to metaphors and help students go beyond the literal in understanding what they are reading and writing about. What better way is there to ensure that the basics are taught in depth, than to include the basic intellectual tools and symbol systems—reinforced through exploratory computer-based instruction?

The Future of Human–Machine Interaction

The 1990s will bring increasingly powerful multimedia computers into the educational system. Many schools have already connected their computers to videodisc players and CD-ROM devices, and to modems for telecommunication. The synthesis of visual, auditory, and manual cues goes along with the new emphasis on empowering students and teachers. We already have more technology and software than we know how to use. Once teachers have a chance to figure out how to use them, these computer-based technological tools can help creativity and inventiveness permeate all aspects of a child's learning. The process requires fresh metaphors and fresh pedagogical ideas to cope with the computerization that is transforming our educational environment.

As tomorrow's schools struggle with social change, new technology, a rapidly expanding knowledge base, and a multicultural school population, there is an ever-increasing need to help students understand basic skills *and* develop higher order thinking abilities. As schools move through the 1990s, computers will be viewed as just one part of the technology equation. The school microcomputers of the early 1980s were the electronic learning equivalent of the worksheet. Computers are now multimedia devices capable of full motion video, voice recognition, interactive graphics, and touch-sensitive screens. With the right software and peripheral devices, PCs can now turn a disk of data into a book (with illustrations) in a few minutes, making high-quality personalized publishing a reality.

The most advanced computers are already starting to incorporate virtual reality programs. The goal of virtual reality engineers is to simulate a landscape ("cyberspace") in which it is possible to walk around and manipulate computer-generated objects at will (Rheingold, 1991). These programs set up artificial worlds that allow the user to put on gloves and goggles (that are attached to the computer), view things in three dimensions, and interact with the world from new vantage points (as a frog or bird, for example). Between Nintendo and the MIT Media Lab there is no telling what students will be using at home in the 1990s.

The computer monitor is already bringing us more than print and simple graphics. Multimedia or hypermedia information combines moving video, sound, animation, and printed words. Programs like Apple's *HyperCard* allow information to be set up in a way that allows different learning styles to be accommodated. Using these programs, learners can selectively hop down a variety of learning alleys as they fluidly move through subjects. As users communicate and weave knowledge in their personal way, they will need new, more flexible thinking skills to create their own multimedia works, interact with literature, and absorb elements of the symbolic world when they are made concrete by an energizing technology. We live in a multimedia world, and teachers need to be able to use each medium to its full advantage.

Electronic communications doesn't have to be a retreat from substance. The evidence suggests that technological vehicles can be a critical tool for supporting human relationships and interaction. The same technology used to teach children can also be used to assist in connecting with parents and teaching teachers throughout their career. Another wave of possibility may be approaching. Technology has a potential for individualizing instruction and providing support for the commitment, caring, and concern that teachers feel about students.

Being able to ride new waves of possibilities when they appear requires intelligent educators ready to help in the creation process. New curricular possibilities can brighten America's bleak learning ground with their unusualness. Using technology to collaboratively connect learning locations and build on interdisciplinary themes is a natural part of the process of making today's curriculum more meaningful.

As we all work to manage our own learning—both present and future—the ability to creatively think and solve problems cooperatively will become more important than ever. Working creatively with technology means examining the possibilities for the cooperative improvement of computer-based education. There is a great battle that must be fought against ignorance, intolerance, and indifference. And computer technology will be a useful electronic partner.

Language makes us human. Literacy, numeracy, and art make us civilized. Science and technology make us powerful.
—D. Adams

REFERENCES

Becker, H. J. (1986). Our national report card: Preliminary results from the new Johns Hopkins survey. *Classroom Computer Learning, 6*(4), 30-3.

Center for Social Organization of Schools. (1986). *Instructional uses of school computers: Reports from the 1985 national survey.* Baltimore, MD: The Johns Hopkins University.

Cole, M., Griffin, P., & Laboratory of Comparative Human Cognition. (1987). *Contextual factors in education: Improving science and mathematics education for minorities and women.* Prepared for the Committee on Research in Mathematics, Science and Technology Education. Madison, WI: National Research Council.

Costanzo, W. (1989). *The electronic text: Learning to write, read, and reason with computers.* Englewood Cliffs, NJ: Educational Technology Publications.

Ede, L., & Lunsford, A. (1986). Why write...together: A research update. *Rhetoric Review, 5*(1), 71-81.

Franklin, S. (1987). *Making the literature, writing, word processing connection: The best of the Writing Notebook 1983-1987.* Mendocino, CA: The Writing Notebook.

Gardner, H., & Perkins, D. (Eds.). (1989). *Art, mind and education: Research from project zero.* Ithaca, NY: University of Illinois Press.

Goldenberg, E.P., & Wallace, F. (1987). *Exploring language with logo.* Cambridge, MA: MIT Press.

Kloosterman, P., Ault, P., & Harty, H. (1985). School-based computer education: Practices and trends. *Educational Technology, 25*(5), 35-38.

Maddux, C.D., & Johnson, D.L. (1988). *Logo: Methods and curriculum for teachers.* New York: Haworth Press.

Mandell, C.J., & Mandell, S.L. (1989). *Computers in education today.* St. Paul, MN: West Publishing Co.

The Office of Technology Assessment, U.S. Congress. (1988). *Power on! New tools for teaching and learning.* Washington, DC: U.S. Government Printing Office.

Pea, R., & Sheingold, K. (1987). *Mirrors of minds: Patterns of experience in educational computing.* Norwood, NJ: Ablex Publishing Corp.

Rheingold, H. (1991). *Virtual reality.* New York: Summit Books.

Silvern, S.B. (1988). Word processing the writing process. In J.L. Hoot & S. B. Lilvern (Eds.), *Writing with computers in the early grades.* New York: Teachers College Press.

Solomon, C. (1986). *Computer environments for children: A reflection on theories of learning and education.* Cambridge, MA: MIT Press.

Vedder, P.H. (1985). *Cooperative learning: A study on processes and effects of cooperation between primary school children.* The Hague: Stichting Voor Onderzoek van net Onderwijs.

Yerushalmy, M., Chazan, D., & Gorden, M. (1987). *Guided inquiry and technology: A year long study of children and teachers using the Geometric Supposer* (Tech. Rep. No. 88-6). Cambridge, MA: Educational Technology Center, Harvard University Graduate School of Education.

Young, R. (1990). *A critical theory of education: Habermas and our children's future.* New York: Teachers College Press.

MULTIMEDIA RESOURCES

Activision. (1989). *The Manhole and Cosmic Osmo.* 3885 Bahannon Drive, Menlo Park, CA 94025.

Addison Wesley Publishing Company. (1990). An early edition of the new series. *Macintosh Inside Out.*

Advent Computer Products. *The Neotech Image Grabber* provides quality 8-bit grayscale or 24-bit color images.

Altsys Corporation. *Fontograper, Fontastic Plus, The Art Importer,* and *Metamorphosis.*

Andromeda Computer Systems, Ltd. *Master Tuner* turns your Macintosh computer into a visual television tuner. (The TV picture shows up as a window.)

Array Technologies, Inc. *Array Scanner-One,* a high-resolution electronic still camera.

Arts Nova Software. *Practica Musica* 2.2, the latest version of this comprehensive music training program for Macintosh.

Articulate Systems, Inc. *The Voice Navigator,* it recognizes any voice, any accent, any language.

Artbeats A tool for desktop publishers, full-page background images in EPS format, including Dimensions, Natural Images, Potpourri.

B&B Soundworks. (1989). *A Country Christmas.* 1040 S. Daniel Way, San Jose, CA 90025.

Ceres Software, Inc. *Inspiration, The Thought Processor,* combines fast and easy visual diagramming and powerful outlining.

Encyclopedia Britannica Educational Corporation. *Compton's Multimedia Encyclopedia.* Britannica Centre, 310 South Michigan Ave. Chicago, IL 60604.

Creative Software. *Easy Color Paint,* a high-quality, low-cost 256 color painting program for the Macintosh.

Cultural Resources. (1989). *Culture 1.1.* 7 Little Falls Way, Scotch Plains, NJ 07076.

Digital Vision, Inc. A new full-color version of Computer Eves, a low-cost, high-quality video digitizer for the Mac II.

Eastgate Systems. (1988). *Presidential Election of 1912.* PO Box 1307, Cambridge, MA 02238.

Institute for Research in Information and Scholarship. (1986). *Intermedia.* Brown University, Box 1946, Providence, RI 02912.

Mass Microsystems, Colorspace technology.

Reactor, CD-ROM full of stimulating art and animation.

Voyager Company, (1988). *Amanda Stories.* 2139 Manning, Los Angeles, CA 90025.

Xiphias. (1988). *Time Table of History.* 13464 Washington Boulevard, Marina Del Rey, CA 90292.

6

COLLABORATION, CREATIVITY, AND ART EDUCATION

When love, creativity, and skill work together—expect a masterpiece.
—John Ruskin

Creativity seems to be deeply rooted in how a child's early symbolic products convey meaning (Applebee, Langer, & Mullis, 1987). Even very young children can describe, interpret, and evaluate their visual perceptions of the world. Later creative efforts often draw on such early art and aesthetic endeavors. Social groups can encourage or inhibit the creative response. Creativity is not limited to the young or groups of people referred to as "creative." In fact it has been suggested that creativity is part of our biological nature, because most people are capable of creativity and most people's creative abilities can be enhanced (Smith, 1990).

Creativity involves a certain flexibility of mind and a willingness to change ideas in midstream if something isn't working out. At times it involves trusting the less acceptable way of doing something, daringly taking plain parts and creating an unforgettable whole. At other times the ability to look at problems directly and the willingness to take a chance (on a hunch) can also produce effective surprises. Thus, creative work frequently requires an element of risk taking—running against the prevailing winds. This means going beyond the sure footing of expertise or experience to deal with unintended consequences.

Creativity in any realm rarely occurs from scratch, or as a result of step-by-step preplanning. More frequently it involves putting things together that haven't been connected before—a combination of choices within a particular area. Most breakthroughs didn't come from working towards a specific goal, but from the actual process of growing attuned to what was going on in an environment that stimulated the reach for innovative solutions (Gardner, 1982).

There also seems to be a link between altering perspective and the creative process. The plant on the window ledge is just a decoration until it sprouts a bud and opens to reveal its flower. A bug is a silly nuisance until we capture it, focus attention, an discover its properties. What we do aesthetically *does* have consequences for our social lives. On both a personal and social level there is a direct link between heightened creativity, vision, and cultural purpose. Becoming more curious and less complacent can foster the coming together of courage, purpose, hope, strength, and imagination.

The Processes of Creative Thinking

Creative thinking is natural human process that can be amplified by awareness and practice. All students can learn to practice creative thinking and engage in the creative process. Creative processes are the fundamental dimensions of thinking, essential tools for achieving many objectives in the real world. Some of these processes have been identified as:

1. *Forming concepts*—establishing ideas, building essential mental construct
2. *Making generalizations*—describing relationships that can be applied to multiple examples.
3. *Extracting new information from a variety of sources and integrating it with what is already known*—comprehension
4. *Problem solving*—a step-by-step process of arriving at an unknown solution or solving a dilemma
5. *Decision making*—choosing or inventing the best alternative based on some criteria
6. *Engaging in scientific inquiry*—describing phenomena, formulating, and testing hypotheses, explaining, predicting
7. *Composing*—creating and developing a product
8. *Practicing oral discourse*verbal interaction, inventive dialogue between two or more people

Although creative thinking processes are needed to form the base, that knowledge is useful only to the degree it can be applied or used to create new knowledge. Thus students need opportunities to collaboratively use their knowledge, compose, make decisions, solve problems, and conduct research to discover and create new knowledge (Hofstadter, 1985). To accomplish these objectives students need instruction and practice in a number of creative thinking skills, such as:

1. *Focusing*—attending to selected chunks of information, defining, identifying key concepts, recognizing the problem, and setting goals

2. *Information gathering*—becoming aware of the substance of content needed; observing, obtaining information, forming questions, clarifying through inquiry

3. *Remembering*—activities involving information storage and retrieval. Encoding and recalling are thinking skills which have been found to improve retention. These skills involve strategies such as rehearsal, mnemonics, visualization, and retrieval.

4. *Organizing*—arranging information to that it can be understood or presented more effectively. Some of these organizing skills consist of comparing, classifying (categorizing) ordering, and representing information.

5. *Analyzing*—These skills are used in classifying and examining in formation of components and relationships. Analysis is at the heart of critical thinking. Recognizing and articulating attributes and components parts, focusing on details and structure, identifying relationships and patterns, grasping the main idea, and finding errors are elements of analysis.

6. *Integrating*—putting things together, solving, understanding, forming principles, and creating composition. These thinking strategies involve summarizing, combined information, deleting unnecessary material, graphically organizing, outlining, and restructuring to incorporate new information.

7. *Evaluating*—assessing the reasonableness and quality of ideas. Skills of evaluation include establishing criteria and proving or verifying date (Perkins, Lockhead, & Bishop, 1987).

These thinking skills appear almost spontaneously, especially among proficient learners. Most of these skills can be enhanced by effective instructional conditions and methods. There is strong evidence that many students (especially the younger and lower achievers) need explicitly and sustained instruction to become skilled in thinking and monitoring their own thinking processes (Bossert, 1989). Teaching students how to *think* throughout the life-long learning process is a key element in any curriculum.

It is important to make students aware of the characteristics of creative and critical thinking and provide experiences for its application. True problem solving involves identifying central questions, posing group strategies for solution, evaluating alternative possibilities, and developing a plan for implementing the best solution.

Group discussion and shared decision making are intricately entwined in the process. Through the practice of cooperative group work a number of creative thinking strategies can come together. There is a great deal of truth in the adage that you remember 15% of what you hear, 30% of what you hear and see, and 60% of what you hear, see, and do. And you remember 80% of what you hear, see, do, and teach others.

Students need a chance to conceptualize and formulate their own purposes and explore problems of their own choosing. At the start of the creative process a period of ambiguity if often helpful in opening up a wider range of possibilities. Frequently, thing don't turn out as planned. Ideas can be changed in the works—revision is one of the keys to quality. The time for executing critical judgment and drawing some of the interdisciplinary connections can come on later drafts. In fact viewing something as a "work in progress" can often help get the creative juices flowing.

It is important for teachers to engage learners in the active exploration of ideas. When this happens students are much more likely to find learning exciting and fun. Good teachers try to build on cultural diversity, individual learning styles, and collaboration to help students focus on the thinking process, understand, and step outside the boundaries of experience (Goodlad, forthcoming). This means that the teacher and students open themselves to suggestions, criticism, styles of thinking, and connections heretofore unexamined.

Some Suggestions for Fostering Creative Thinking

- Provide opportunities for groups of students to explore different view points and examine both sides of an issue.
- Conduct debates and discussions on controversial issues. Students work in groups to present an argument on a topic and explain their view to another group. Sides can then be switched and the opposite view defended.
- Encourage students to ask open-ended questions like *How were time zones set up? Who was against it and why? What is the relationship between ends and means?* Let small groups of students come up with the possibilities and share with the whole class.
- Have the class brainstorm a list of interests or categories that they feel themselves or others are good at. Place pieces of paper with the numbers 1 through 4 up (in different places). As the item is called, have students stand in front of the number (4—excellent, 1—poor) that corresponds to their view of how good at something they believe they are at activities brainstormed such as swimming, sewing, handling money, cooking, dancing, reading, working in groups, painting, . . . The purpose is to help the students see that everyone is talented in something and nobody is great at everything. The folk saying, "List for the music only you can play, and play it," applies here.

The Teacher's Changing Role in Structuring Collaboration

Teachers hold the key to unlocking worlds within common experiences. Making them all sing the same tune is not what cooperative learning, professional empowerment, and school-based management is all about. Timid approaches and uncertainty about subject matter have long been unspoken hindrances to exciting problem exploration. Many limitations are self-imposed. Often afraid to try a new art, music, or literature activity, teachers frequently fail to exhibit creative inventive strategies. Fearful attitudes and misdirected ideas about accountability create a burden of dutiful textbook lessons that remove most elements of personalization and charm from the process. Is skill-based instruction at fault? Partly so, but mindsets seem to play an even larger role. The total picture (the holistic experience) is attended to when students connect with reading, art, music, and movement.

New aesthetic approaches that involve literature, music, movement and art are eagerly embraced by young learners. If students are excited about what they are learning it is most likely to be a good learning environment. In the same spirit, students are not asked to memorize a paragraph but to infer and connect ideas to their larger personal experience with questions like: *Has anything like this ever happened to you? Why did the character act that way? What you think will happen next? Why did you like it? Do you think that could really happen?* Students should work with a partner or small group to come up with answers—and improve on the questions.

In many subject matter disciplines open-ended questions frequently go unasked. The creativity and spontaneity of the moment are impeded by a "right answer," because many teachers feel they must get preset answers. To implement more imaginative approaches, teachers and parents need to examine their own beliefs about human intelligence, thinking and creativity.

The general problems and the problems of stirring the creativity of children are complex, subtle, and not easy to solve quickly. Sincere personal encouragement by teachers can ignite imaginative performance. False praise, or praise for inferior work, can actually restrict opportunities for creative, thoughtful expression. So can focusing most creativity efforts on the so called "gifted" in schools. The idea that only the gifted and talented should engage in creative effort leads to many students being deprived of the right to be seen in a creative light.

It is difficult to consider products of the imagination apart from the system of values brought to it. Good exercises in art education involve students in altering familiar (or unfamiliar) images along lines they feel are promising. Students need the chance to try things out, reflect on what they have done, and try again. Most teachers know how to encourage or reorient students if they are not making progress on their own. Good teachers also believe all children will learn; they recognize the need for high expectations as they strive to reach every individual To achieve this, it's important to know the subject well enough to feel comfortable with it and be able to draw on additional information, examples, and alternative approaches for those students who were unable to connect with the information.

With dozens of subjects to teach at the elementary level, we are fortunate to have teachers with enough artistic knowledge and skill to teach painting, pottery, music, media literacy, and movement. Exploring the broad philosophical dimensions of art will have to be the next step. Teaching expanded lists of facts and bits of knowledge of little use unless they're integrated into a larger whole. With inspired teaching and hard work today's students can develop artistic sensitivity and reasoning skill that touches other subjects.

Effective teachers strive to insure what's being learned is a center of interest for students. This often means walking a fine line as they engage students as active thinkers—without interfering when children are working well on their own. Fortunately the best way to approach a creative experience in the arts is to provide an opportunity to explore it. Informed adult encouragement, when it's available needs to recognize, like Emerson, that is is often best to "let the bird sing without deciphering the song.

New Assessment Methods

The experiences we bring to the world all contribute to the accuracy of our perception of reality. While thinking about these schools may now be sufficiently radical to improve education it would be a serious mistake if a primitive technology of evaluation is allowed to drive our educational goals. To change the schools for the better, we will have to design evaluation instruments that are consistent *with the aims* of the desired change. To understand the educational process, we must get information from multiple sources: the observation of teachers the community, classroom life, work samples, and gleaning information from students about what's going on.

For cooperative learning to achieve its potential, assessment procedures need to connect to deep educational values. Standardized tests don't do a good job of measuring student creativity of achievement; thus, teachers are starting to place more emphasis on student work samples and group projects to measure the work being done. Teachers are also experimenting with peer editing, group criticism, and active learning teams.

Portfolios, open-ended questions, holistic grading of writing, and interactive responses are some possibilities being explored. Portfolios can include art work, computer programs, writing, and even student-produced VCR tapes. Video discs or computer simulations can provide students with realistic situations and real problems to solve.

Teachers and students need to be part of a caring community of learners that uses every assessment tool with promise. Choosing better evaluation instruments requires looking at how children learn and trusting the teacher to be an informed decision maker. It does not good to learn inductively and then test on convergent thinking. Most of the serious problems in American education cannot be solved by more of the same: *more* testing, *more* homework, *more* time-on-task, *more* required courses, or *more* school days.

ENCHANCING THE QUALITY OF ARTS EDUCATION THROUGH COLLABORATION

Art flourishes where there is a sense of adventure.
—Alfred North Whitehead

Advancing the understanding, cultures, art, creativity, and human values has everything to do with the life and quality of this nation. Nevertheless educational decision makers in the United States have generally not paid much attention to these issues. At best, they are found on the fringes of the American school curriculum. This is due in part to not having a long tradition of prizing artistic expression in children. Little is expected of our citizens or our leaders when it comes to knowledge about artistic forms. The United States spends nearly $50 billion a year on science and much less than $1 billion on all the humanities put together (Kaagan, 1990). Still, amid dire concerns, there are glimmers of optimism. There is a vague feeling that the arts can open new horizons, enrich the spirit, and help educate students to expand an American cultural vision.

In many of our schools there is an unfortunate tendency to view the arts as an emotional extension rather than a cognitive discipline with a knowledge base and social, historical, and philosophical roots. Since the arts are often seen as a personal luxury and not associated with "real wage-earning" occupations, developing or maintaining a good arts education program is very difficult. Such programs, if they have any funding to begin with, are most vulnerable to budget cuts. And while money doesn't always solve education problems, it can make a critical difference when it comes to making the arts a vital universe for thought, action and exploring complacencies.

Human societies have always depended on the arts to give insight into truths, however painful or unpopular they may be. Today, in many countries, there is wide agreement that the arts can aid children in developing creativity while becoming good citizens and productive workers. The basic notion is that the world is poorer without the arts. A country's richness of knowledge, enlightenment, and enduring resources for research also benefits from artistic endeavor. From Asia to Europe, art education is one of the central features of the school curriculum. Americans are beginning to take notice.

Building the future for education in art means expanding the links within the arts and the education communities. There is a visual world out there that youngsters must explore if they are to be broadly educated and develop critical-thinking, problem-solving, and imagination skills. All of these creative-thinking qualities can be taught and reinforced, helping children integrate the skills of producing critiques and reflecting on aesthetic concerns.

Creativity and Aesthetic Criticism.

Children frequently have the ability to do creative work in the arts. What's missing is the opportunity for expression and analysis. When students do have the chance to express themselves, there is the excitement of producing in their own way and conveying personal experience. They are capable of using figurative language (metaphors, similes, etc.) in their writing and symbolism in their painting. The challenge is to encourage meaningful concepts and images to emerge.

Children can be involved in artistic interdisciplinary projects—ranging from illustrating their own books to producing videos with camcorders. Process are production are important elements. But the historical and critical dimensions of art education are just as important. To understand literature, for example, children must function as critics. The same thing is true for art. They are cognitive activities that connect the various dimensions of a subject. The creative effect of questioning, challenging, and aesthetic reflection all contribute to creative habits of mind. An individual's creativity rarely reaches across all subjects. More often it occurs with a domain of knowledge. Whatever the area of special interest and skill, an understanding of the arts can help children develop their special gifts (Eisner, 1990).

Including Art Education in School Reform

Art is communication spoken by man for humanity in a language raised above the everyday happening.
　　　　—Mary Wigman

In an effort to make arts education part of the national curriculum reform, a series of *Discipline Based Art Education* reports has been put forward by the Getty Foundation (1989). Schools are encouraged to help students go beyond creating to art criticism, history, and aesthetics. In some of these projects art educators, historians, philosophy professors and local teachers collaborate to make aesthetics less mysterious for children and young adults. Even at early levels students need to be grounded in the ability to reflect on art and be able to think about the thinking skills involved.

Although the connection to a rich artistic tradition is important, no response should be considered *the* "right" one. In fact, seeking the rewards of what adults see as good creative products, often makes their appearance less likely. Instead, teachers can mix modeling intellectual stimulation with the natural rapport that is such an important part of the mysterious art of good teaching (Bowers & Finders, 1990).

Art criticism, history, and aesthetics contribute to production and a child's ability to draw inferences and interpret the powerful ideas. Art (like television, reading or mathematics) makes use of certain conventions and symbol systems to express figurative meaning. It can include symbols in its expression through style (the fine detail), composition (arrangement of elements), and by creating the possibility for multiple meanings. "Reading" an artist's symbols is as much of a skill as reading print or video images.

Art means going beyond the transient messages that are often overvalued by the culture (Beane, 1990). In a multicultural society like the United States, it also means weaving artistic material from other cultures into the curriculum, enabling students to confirm creatively the truth and beauty of their heritage. Art is not limited to specific times of cultures. Greek art learned from Egypt. Christian art was shaped by ideas from Greece and the East. African, Chinese, Egyptian, and Mexican art have influenced Modernism. Students find artists responding to almost any conceivable visual source and tradition as they deal with real questions from today's art world such as: Is the whole notion of "quality" in art a European notion? Is it sometimes valid to emphasize content rather than form?

Exposing children to a variety of artistic forms and materials will make it easier to locate areas of strength and weakness. All students may have a similar range of choices, but it is how these choices are made that count. Choosing from a variety of artistic and intellectual possibilities is beneficial for building both the strength of creativity and basic skills. In addition, the arts can also help get a dialogue going between subject matter areas are brought together, the result can be a new and valuable way of look at the world.

New Collaborative Strategies for Teaching the Arts

To explore art education often requires building teams and providing structure so that each group has a range of student abilities and teachers can join in the quest for better understanding. Teachers can also be formed into small peer groups so that they can share their new insights with other teachers. New teachers, in particular, need to be exposed to extraordinary (experienced) teachers. Joint ventures can encourage creativity in the arts by modeling an approach to problems and materials without instilling structured rules or emphasizing imitation. In the final analysis it is the teacher who must balance the conflicting calls for art or basic skills.

Valuing a range of contributions within a supportive and collaborative community can make the difference between a competent self-image and the devastating belief that nothing can be done "right." Recasting the teacher's role from authority figure dispensing knowledge to that of a collaborative decision maker is a major ingredient in the process. Making students active participants in deciding what and how they should learn doesn't diminish the need for informed adult leadership. Rewarding students for collective reasoning, and using each other as resources, can foster a sense of community.

The teacher helps students gain confidence in their ability and the group's ability to work through problems and place less reliance on the teacher for validating their thinking. This involves a conceptual reexamination of today's student population, the learning process, decision-making relationships, and classroom organizational structure. The challenge of the professional teacher in this new environment is:

- to take a more active role in serving student of multicultural backgrounds and "at-risk" students. In many cases this means addressing non-Western art.
- to focus and take advantage of cooperative learning teams to foster students' thinking, reasoning, and problem-solving abilities.
- to make use of cooperative learning strategies, peer tutoring, and new technology to reach a range of learners and learning styles.
- to work to professionalize art education and legitimatize art in the schools. This includes assessment of student knowledge, ability, and performance.
- to develop exemplary materials supportive of cooperative learning. This development will have to be done with particular attention to: the promotion of thinking skills, the needs of "at risk" students, the needs of teacher professionalism, assessment, accountability, and the advent of new technologies.

What is worth teaching? We are stuck with such a rapid growth of knowledge that the notion of educating minds in critical thinking and creative modes of thought is looking ever more appealing.

Creativity and the Vital Role of Arts Education

Improving art education is as connected to improving cultural quality as it is with increasing productivity. Much of what students have to do in the world outside of school involves the ability to work in groups, plan, execute, and complete various kinds of projects. Real-life creativity involves innovative answers to questions and sometimes even changing the nature of the question itself. Fostering creativity in the arts—or anything else—means encouraging students to think for themselves, with group support. This way they can come up with different solutions to problems as they link arts education to their own personal experience.

Children possess the capacity to absorb knowledge—but it takes intelligent teaching to use that knowledge to reason effectively. It is often adult models (like teachers and parents) that make the difference between a commitment to the arts or dismissing them as irrelevant. If we are to create an educational renaissance that so many are calling for, then art education must play a vital role as an agent of social change in general and education in particular.

Getting students interested in a topic or problem and interacting with others in an environment that allows thoughtful and creative expression are objectives that few educators will disagree with. Yet how, with today's already cluttered curriculum and testing requirements, does a teacher find time to unearth topics of interest and excitement for all subject areas?

Some teachers can supply anecdotes about effective teaching: the butterfly that "hatched" from a chrysalis in their classroom, students' creative language experience stories, data observations, creative dramatics, and painting murals. Other teachers might recall the newscast of the whale trapped in the ice which spawned an array of activities: research on whales, letters to elected representatives, a bulletin board chart in bird migration patterns, and an attitude survey graph. Good teachers know that, to be really excited about a subject, they must really care about it.

The social forces surrounding a field of study and individual talent are important factors in generating (or inhibiting) creativity. As far as arts education is concerned, this means legitimizing its goals by becoming an active force in educational change, assuming a more aggressive role with "at-risk" students, and focusing on the potential of the arts to foster thinking skills and problem-solving abilities. To foster creativity in the arts and science requires a conviction that creative expression is more than a frill, going beyond classroom recreation to its recognition as a serious subject.

All social and educational institutions convey messages that can affect creativity and artistic development. Deep questions of value are involved in the kinds of models we set and our methods for evaluating artistic products. Art may belong to everyone, but being literate in the subject mean being able to understand, critique, and crate in a whole array of symbol systems. This means it's desirable to have some basic skill training early on. As children gain more aesthetic understanding, it makes sense to think of them as participants in the artistic process. They can paint their own paintings, jointly compose music, and collaborate in arranging their own dances. This way they can experience the inner nature of how aesthetic creativity develops.

The Interaction Between Basic Skill Knowledge and Creative Thinking

Creativity is more than originality. There is a strong connection between creativity (including originality and novelty) and basic academic skills. The two feed on each other. Developing a unique clarity, style, and focus is essential to any skill area. The goal is not simply to learn subskills but to perfect them so that students can reach toward comprehension. The rote drill approach of educational fundamentalists, and narrow thinking patterns, often get "stuck" in elementary school. At best, proficiency and performance are limited educational objectives. Although there is nothing wrong with teaching subskills, it is equally important to encourage the development of images to flesh out dry facts with substance. Elements of basic skills and creativity (combined with literature, mathematical patterns, and art) open up a multiplicity of images which can be creatively tapped and explored.

Many agree that encouraging creative behavior is as important for our society as mastering the basic skills. And there is general agreement that it should be encouraged in the classroom. There is plenty of disagreement, however, over the curriculum focus and how to go about fostering creative skills. The traditional notion of educators is that, if fluency, flexibility, and originality were systematically taught, true creativity would follow. Unfortunately, it isn't that simple. To begin with, teachers didn't know how to teach it or model these concepts. Secondly, fluency doesn't count for much if all the ideas generated are simply novel or trivial. Worse yet, if flexibility clouds issues or discourages student decision making, it can impede learning. Even "originality," as it's understood in this context, is sometimes simple social accommodation rather than either intuitive boundary pushing or barrier breaking.

Traditionally, common school practice encouraged children to be plodders who saw the rules as conduits for action rather than as springboards for changing realities. Taking risks, dealing with failure, the desire to be surprised, and enjoying ambiguity are all essential elements in creative behavior. All are difficult for teachers to teach and model, *and* for many students to accept. After all, simply accepting the "Imperial Mandate" from someone in authority helps one avoid the fatigue of figuring things out for oneself.

In the real world we learn a lot about creativity from our failures, accidents, and the personal restructuring of our reality in the face of uncertainty. Taking risks in a nonjudgmental environment, making mistakes, and "debugging the program" are just a few element of computing which can create an atmosphere where creativity can flourish. There are elements of fluency, novelty, originality, flexibility, intuition, and personal decision making involved in building creative models. But we also need to go beyond literal understandings.

Schools have always found it easier to stimulate literal thinking that to stress inventiveness. Although both arts education and creativity have been formalized as curriculum goals—and included in the education debate—we are just beginning to see serious attention given to actually implementing these concerns in the classroom. There is general agreement that the arts must be part of a teacher's preserve and in-service program if we are to translate them into a comprehensive curriculum.

Arts education curriculum developers and teachers are facing the challenge of somehow fusing creative thinking to basic skills. Several researchers suggest that simply providing a rich artistic environment helps, because there is usually enough structure in a student's mind to search out interesting material (Smith, 1990). To go much further requires a skillful teacher who examines the quality of the thought that has gone into student productions and helps students with critical analysis and self-cultivation. With all their other problems and curriculum dependence, can schools successfully add to their lists?

Some American education institutions have proven that they can design learning experiences that, in the arts, are optimal for a diversity of learning styles and student dispositions. They do this by assisting students in developing both disciplined basic skills and genuine creativity, thus providing multiple paths for student development (Gardner, 1990). As students gain creative observational skills, they can develop distinctive styles and gain familiarity with a wide range of artistic approaches.

Without the arts, students would be denied access to the opportunity to develop the mental skills that make art possible and gain access to a vast cultural legacy. Art is more than some arbitrary abstract notion of beauty. Good art helps us rethink our conception of reality and alters our perspective. It can also be a very effective source of inspiration for connecting diverse subjects. The creativity engendered by art can be a catalyst for information, change, and the enrichment of our intellectual, cultural, and civic life.

REFERENCES

Applebee, J., Langer, A., & Mullis, I. (1987). *Learning to be literate in America: Reading, writing and reasoning.* Princeton, NJ: National Association of Educational Progress, Educational Testing Service.

Beane, J.A. (1990). *Affect in the curriculum: Toward democracy, dignity, and diversity.* New York: Teachers College Press.

Bossert, S.T. (1989). Cooperative activities in the classroom. In E.Z. Rothkopf (Ed.), *Review of research in education.* Washington, DC: AERA.

Bowers, C.A., & Finders, D.J. (1990). *Responsive teaching: An ecological approach to patterns, language, cultural and thought.* New York: Teachers College Press.

Eisner, E. (1990) *The enlightened eye.* New York: Macmillan.

Gardner, H. (1982). *Art, mind and brain: A cognitive approach to creativity.* New York: Basic Books.

Gardner, H. (1990). *To open minds.* Basic Books: New York.

Getty Center for Education In the Arts. (1989). *Education in art: Future building.* New York: Author.

Goodlad, J. (1990). *Teachers for the nation's schools.* Seattle, WA: Center for Education Renewal, University of Washington.

Hofstadter, D. (1985). *Metamagical themes: Questing for the essence of mind and pattern.* New York: Basic Books.

Kaagan, S. (1990). *Aesthetic persuasion: Pressing the cause of arts education in American schools.* A Monograph for the Gety Center for Education in the Arts.

Perkins, D.N., Lockhead, J., & Bishop, J. (1987). *Transfer and teaching thinking.* Hillsdale, NJ: Erlbaum.

Smith, R. (Ed.). (1990). *Discipline-based art education: Origins, meaning and development.* Champagne, IL: University of Illinois Press.

7

THEMATIC APPROACHES

Pushing Beyond Subject Matter
Limits

The world of work and education are increasingly specialized. Paradoxically, individuals are called upon to overcome subject matter boundaries in order to synthesize information and jointly formulate creative solutions to problems. Solving problems in any domain assumes collaborative interpersonal skills and an natural link between domains of knowledge.

The various disciplines are not natural entities; rather, they are useful frameworks created to make sense of a part of the world. As such they are the artifacts of a particular culture, refined to serve a useful function at a particular point in time. Pushing beyond these artificial limits is often more productive than reaching for the most convenient discipline-based conclusions. In the real world there is usually a need for multiple interpretations and building bridges between subjects. How can the classroom reflect these real life concerns?

The arts and humanities have proved very useful tools for integrating curricular areas and helping students transcend narrow subject matter concerns (The College Board, 1985). Teachers have often used visual imagery and intellectual tools from the fine arts as a thematic lens for examining diverse subjects. Some schools have even worked out an integrated school day, where interdisciplinary themes add interest, meaning, and function to collaboration. Mathematics, writing, science, music, art appreciation, and reading can all be wrapped around a central theme, making rich connections which stimulate the mind and the senses.

The research suggests that using thematic approach improves students' knowledge of subject matter and aids in transfer. An additional finding is that good units that are organized around themes can improve the students' abilities to apply their knowledge to new subjects (Sharan, 1990). In art, for example, language development flourishes when children are encouraged to discuss the materials they are using and reflect on the nature of their art work through writing. Whatever the combination, an important result of integrating various subjects around a theme is a gain in thinking and learning skills—*The metacurriculum* (Wlodkowski & Jaynes, 1990).

The Imaginative Linking of subjects

Before we can deal with teaching the thinking process, children need something solid to think about. After that teachers need to provide continuity between activities and subjects. The thinking skills engendered in one area can serve as a connection between subjects. While watching a newscast about whales trapped in the ice, one fifth-grade class decided to find out more about the characteristics of whales, how much they weighed, their migratory patterns, and what led to their status as an endangered species. In the process their research they did mathematical calculations, explored geographical, historical, and social issues, and generated their own ideas and solutions to the problem.

In linking subjects or pulling connection metaphors from different fields, a couple of problems kept cropping up for teachers: Many felt uncomfortable with material out of their field, and when interdisciplinary work took time away from "their" subject some felt that their area of expertise was being undervalued (Carnegie Foundation for the Advancement of Teaching, 1988). Collegial support provided the impetus for overcoming these problems.

In making curriculum connections, it's often helpful for teachers to see model lessons that include cross-disciplinary suggestions and activities. The relationships established between subject and the way teachers facilitate these relationships are important. When disciplines are integrated around a central concept, students can practice the skills that they have learned from many subjects. This helps students make sense out of the world (Maeroff, 1988).

Whether it's art, reading, social studies, mathematics, or science, learning can be a connected creative process. As teachers learn to link subjects in imaginative ways, they must also look for information *within students* that it can be related to. By opening communication channels at a personal level, connections can be made with knowledge students already have. Once the teacher gets to know the student, it is easier to bring diverse groups and perspectives together to solve problems.

To successfully link subjects and accommodate a plurality of student interests, abilities, and cultures, teachers need to be in touch with both their students and the social milieu of the community. The teaching and learning process in any culture, in large part, is based on social beliefs about how students learn and what they should know. Learning can flourish for everybody in a teacher-initiated learning community where creative and sustained effort gives every student a measure of acceptance and success (Sigley & Anderson, 1990).

Making Themes a Part of the Curriculum

In the schools, narrow subject matter concerns have sometimes limited the development of the skills necessary for learning content, thinking independently, and applying what has been learned. Isolated subjects can also be devoid of personal interest (Middleton, 1990). Building instructional units around themes can help by encouraging students to think in a manner that gives them a framework in which to synthesize their personal and educational experiences. When students see that teachers are really trying to help them get wherever they want to go, they see themselves as important. Students are more likely to succeed if they have a sense of their own possibilities (Csikszentmihalyi & Csikszentmihalyi, 1988).

The goal of a interdisciplinary curriculum is to bring to together different perspectives so that diverse intellectual tools can be applied to a common theme, issue or problem. Thematic approaches can help by providing a group experience that fosters thinking and learning skills that will serve students in the larger world. By its very definition, *interdisciplinary* implies cooperation among disciplines and people. The notion that students of different abilities and backgrounds can learn from each other is a natural outgrowth of the collaborative tendency inherent in this approach. Everyone's collaborative involvement not only allows input into the planning process, but can help with self-responsibility and long-term commitment to learning (Fraser, 1990).

Organizing parts of the curriculum around themes means that each subject is mutually reinforcing and connected to life-long learning. Subjects from the Greek classics to radiation theory need the historical, philosophical, and aesthetic perspective afforded by interdisciplinary connections. Curriculum integration provides active linkages between areas of knowledge and consciously applies language and methods from more than one discipline to examine a central theme, issue, topic, or experience. This holistic approach focuses on themes and problems and deals with them more in depth rather than memorizing facts and covering the text from cover to cover.

There is always the danger of watering down content in an attempt to cover all areas. We can, however, teach the work of Newton with an eye to the history of the times, the arts, the values, the role of literature, religion, and science—rather than simply compiling isolated facts. The history of ideas, political movements, and changing relationships among people are part of the fabric of our world. We cannot narrowly train people in specialist areas and expect them to be able to deal with the multifaceted nature of 21st-century jobs. Enriching any area of work increasingly requires a connection to a diversity of fields and the ability to continue learning.

A Collaborative interdisciplinary Curriculum Means:

1. *Active Learning*
   Students exchange ideas when they are involved in well organized tasks, with materials they can manipulate. Active learning is enhanced when students can collaboratively make predictions, find patterns, and explore and construct ideas, models, and stories (Dill, 1990).
2. *Interesting Activities*
   Lessons should include activities that are designed to develop higher thinking skills, rather than quick right answers. Problems on diverse topics, which encourage speculation or estimation, are more likely to motivate and encourage students to work together on the lesson.
3. *Chances for Student Interaction*
   Students need to develop the ability to work together, to become sensitive and responsive to group members and group needs. There is a need for activities that involve all group members, as well as a need to sensitize the group to include all members in active involvement.
4. *Opportunities for Thinking*
   Students should be given opportunities to explore diverse ideas emphasizing concepts and relationships. Challenging tasks and opportunities for interaction with peers can lead to more advanced thinking and creative discussions.
5. *Teachers as Advisors and Curriculum Developers*
   Textbooks and teacher's manuals need to be altered or replaced by teacher ideas, materials, an activities that arouse student interest and encourage cooperation (Gage & Berliner, 1990). The teacher's role becomes that of a consultant, advisor, and learner who interacts with teaching peers.
6. *Lesson Structure and Accountability*
   Opportunities should be provided for group- or teacher-led summaries of important aspects of the tasks. Students need to discuss what they have learned with the teacher and other students in order to understand and explain the activities they have worked on.

Another important aspect of an interdisciplinary approach is cooperative learning and group investigation. Students are encouraged to take an active role in planning what they will study and how they will do it. One way to divide the class is to have students self-select into cooperative groups based on common interests in a topic. Students decide on what specifically they wish to find out, divide up the work among themselves, summarize, and present their findings to the class. There is much freer communication and greater involvement when students share in the planning and decision making and carry out *their* plan. Students achieve more through discussing, investigating, and working in mixed-ability groups than if working alone (Richardson & Skinner, 1990).

Potential Results of Integrating the Curriculum

Learning is social and interconnected. Children learn in the classroom through interaction with their teachers, parents, and one another. This back-and-forth human exchange about the curriculum provides motivation and excitement, helps children to be engaged in their learning, and supports them in their struggles to learn what they need and want to know. This includes developing a sense of how complicated many problems are and the need to adopt multiple perspectives in order to develop a full understanding of complex issues. Asking interconnected questions—and making correlations between subjects, principles, and contexts—is a necessary part of learning in a modern age.

A broad perspective can amplify basic subject matter and help students and teachers become better cooperative thinkers and decision makers. The integration of diverse subjects has advantages sufficient to encourage the examination of what content best lends itself to this approach. Like any concept for organizing learning, the value of interdisciplinary curriculum lies in the quality of the implementation. It always comes back to teachers and their knowledge of their discipline—*the characteristics of effective instruction.* Like E. B. White, who wrote that he wanted to keep the minutes of his own meeting, teachers must learn to script their own lesson plans.

Structuring Cooperative Classrooms Around Themes

Themes can be viewed as the big ideas that link constructs from various disciplines, integrating concepts that make sense of the total picture. They can be used to integrate ideas at all levels of the curriculum. Through the use of themes, such as "structure" or "change," students can see how parts and pieces of knowledge fit together.

Themes can also direct the design of classroom activities by connecting classroom activities and providing them with a logical sequence and scope of instruction.

One set of steps for developing thematic concepts is to:

1. Determine what students know about a topic before beginning instruction. This is done by careful questioning and discussion.
2. Be sensitive to and capitalize on students' knowledge.

3.　Use a variety of instructional techniques to help students achieve conceptual understanding.
4.　Include all students in discussions and cooperative learning situations.

Thematic instruction values depth over breadth of coverage. The content should be chosen on how well it represents what is currently known in the field and its potential for dynamically making connections (Rogoff, 1990).

Thematic Units

The design of thematic units brings together a full range of disciplines in the school's curriculum: language arts, science, social studies, math, art, physical education, and music. Using a broad range of discipline-based perspectives can result in units that last an hour, a day, a few weeks, or a semester. They are not intended to replace a discipline-based approach but act as supportive structures that foster the comprehensive study of a topic. Teachers can plan their interdisciplinary work around issues and themes that emerge from their ongoing curriculum. Deliberate steps can be taken to create a meaningful and carefully orchestrated program hat is more stimulating and motivating for students and teachers. Of course shorter flexible units of study are easier to do than setting up a semester- or year-long thematic unit.

Collaborative thematic curriculum models require a change in how teachers go about their work. It takes planning and energy to create effective integrated lessons, and more time is often needed for subject matter research because teachers frequently find themselves exploring and teaching new material. Thematic teaching also means planning lessons that use untraditional approaches, arranging for field trips, guest speakers, and special events. Contacting parents, staff members, and community resources who can help expand the learning environment is another factor in teacher's time and planning efforts. Long-range planning and professional development for teachers are other important elements of the process.

Many middle schools have incorporated the idea of blocks or cores where language arts, reading and social studies are combined. A math-science block or humanities core are other examples. Teachers who are discipline specialists team together to teach these blocks that can include numerous combinations.

A Thematic Cooperative Learning Model

The ideas suggested here can be carried out for several days or may extend to several weeks, depending on the topic of investigation chosen. In planning and implementing group investigations, students might move through these stages.

1. *Identify a Topic*

    The topic selected by the teacher should be broad and have many dimensions to trigger a variety of reactions and approaches for study. Presenting a topic such as "How did the age of the dinosaurs differ from the modern age of the mammals?" or "What can we learn from the age of the dinosaurs?" is much better than presenting the topic as "dinosaurs." The topic should be multifaceted and set the tone for the study of social studies, science, math, literature, arts, and so on.

    The teacher stimulates inquiry by acquainting the students with the subject. A variety of sources can be used: brief video clips, short lectures, discussions, text materials, magazines, newspapers, field trips, guest speakers, etc. In this first step students are asked to general questions, discuss ideas in groups, and write down their ideas, topics, and questions of interest. The student questions are then brainstormed in a whole-class setting, listing on the board, synthesized, and classified into topic headings. Individuals then self-select and regroup based on the new category selections under the topic.

2. *Plan*

    Cooperative groups are instructed to formulate a research topic, hypothesis, question, or problem and devise a plan for meeting their objective. Members decide how to proceed. The teacher gives input if asked or presents alternatives to groups having difficulties. The group plan must be written down and meet with the teacher's approval before proceeding.

3. *Carry Out the Plan*

    Group members gather information, collect data, analyze, reach conclusions, evaluate, communicate their findings, and build constructions based on their plan. Frequently plans have to be revised or altered to something more realistic or manageable. Members decide on format and presentations. Each may choose to write up his or her own summary or write a collective report of their findings.

4. *Prepare Presentation, Report, Findings*

    Expectations should be clearly related to the groups. If a chart or construction is part of the plan, parameters should be discussed with the class. Oral presentations may need to be supplemented with visuals, etc. Grading of the group projects should be specified—along with how individual's contributions will be recognized and group efforts will be rewarded.

5. *Deliver Class Presentation and Discussion*

    Time constraints and rules should be reviewed. Class dialogue and observation time should also be presented, discussed, and agreed upon prior to presentation.

6. *Evaluate*

Students need time to evaluate what has been learned, summarize, synthesize, discuss, and reflect on their work and the work of their peers. Throughout a thematic project the teachers has had many opportunities to observe and evaluate student performance, interest, and involvement. Hopefully, questions and discussions have been held with individuals and small groups. The final presentation to the whole class is another part of the evaluation (Jacobs, 1989).

COLLABORATIVE ACTIVITIES FOR THEMATIC LEARNING

A carefully balanced combination of direct instruction, self-monitoring, and active group work helps met diverse student needs. The activities suggested here are designed to encourage higher-order thinking and learning and provide a collaborative vehicle for thematic integration of the curriculum.

Collage Photo Art

Students at all levels can become producers as well as consumers of art. We used a videotape of David Hockney's work from *Art in America*. Hockney, one of today's important artists, spoke (on the videotape) about his work and explained his technique. Students then used cameras to explore Hockney's photo collage technique in their own environment. Student groups can arrange several sets of their photos differently—telling unique stories with different compositions of the same pictures. They can even add brief captions or poems to make more connections to the language arts, social studies, or science. Photographers know the meaning of their pictures depend to a large extent on the words that go with them.

Note: Teachers do need to preview any videos before they are used in the classroom, because some parts may not be appropriate for elementary school children. Teachers can also select particular elements and transfer them from one VCR to another, so only the useful segments are present on the tape used in class.

Examine similarities in folk lore and literature

Have student groups explore myths, folk tales, legends, and fairy tales to look for similarities and differences between people, times and cultures.

Construct a group list, concept map, collage, visual image, or writing that shows these group findings. Students can even take photocopies of major works, paste them down on a large piece of tagboard, and paint on top of them.

Make Use of Biographies

Biographies can provide information about values, motives and accomplishments—acting as role models for students. Historical fiction enables students to gain an appreciation of various author's works and to show literature is not written in isolation. Particular themes such as those in Faust and Prometheus serve as discussion for major themes of mankind.

Focus on Inquiry Skills

Emphasis on inquiry skills and the processes of science has made a significant difference on student knowledge, skills mastery, and attitudes. Problem solving and critical thinking can be taught throughout the curriculum in which the teacher continues to be a learner. Helping regular/special students develop an understanding of inquiry (finding out through hypothesis testing, data collection, reporting, generalizing conclusions, communicating results) is an important intellectual tool which will prove to be a lasting contributing as they move toward life-long learning.

Present the Historical View

To keep children from concluding that everything worth knowing has already been discovered. Present an historical view in such subjects as mathematics, astronomy, literature, art, and so on.

Connect Areas of Learning with Practical Applications

Concepts in subject areas make sense to students when they are applied to real situations. Applications of mathematical concepts, such as probability, are made in insurance, biology, physics, weather forecasting, psychology, social science, and medical research, as well as many sports and recreational activities. Encourage students to explore areas where concepts like these are used. Using resources such as newspapers, outside experts, friends, adults, books, TV programs, and so on, construct a group list of all the ways a concept, like probability is used. Students may give examples and supply resources or references, act out probability scenarios, and so on.

Create Writing Partnerships

A common collaborative learning strategy is to divide the partnership into a "thinker" and a "writer." One partner reads a short concept or question out loud and tells what he or she thinks the answer should be. The writer writes it down if they agree. If not they try to convince the "thinker" that there is a better answer. If agreement cannot be reached they write two answers and initial one.

Brainstorm

In pairs, have students brainstorm a topic; for example, list as many things as you can think of that move, things that are deep, sharp, white, or soft. You may wish to set a 3- or 5-minute time limit.

Generate Ideas: Convergent Thinking

Take a situation in current events or from literature and have students in small groups generate ideas for 10 minutes with judgment deferred. Then take 10 minutes to have the group evaluate their ideas. Instruct group members to make a list of their five best and file silliest ideas to share with the class. (Explain that the most unlikely ideas frequently result in the best solutions.)

Example: take the situation from the Daniel Defoe book *Robinson Crusoe*—put yourself in his situation. Washed ashore on a desert island with nothing but a large belt and belt buckle. How can these tools be used to survive? (a) 10 minutes—generated as many ideas as possible, (b) 10 minutes—to evaluate, (c) Bring the best and funniest back to the whole class.

> ***Group Evaluation Activity.*** Count fluency scores by giving one point for a common response and three points for a creative one. Have each group choose one creative response and expand on that idea by writing a paragraph. Share paragraphs and include them in a class book for others to read. These activities develop students' ability to think divergently, a skill which even many academically gifted students do not have.

Develop Communication Skills Through Oral History

Oral history is a systematic way to obtain from the lips of living Americans a record of their participation in the political, economic, and cultural affairs of the nation. It is a process of collecting reminiscences, accounts, and interpretations of events from the recent past which are of historical significance. As students gather information from people who grew up in a time and manner different from theirs, the students practice their communications skills through collecting, compiling, selecting, and organizing data. Students can construct and compare the experiences of the older Americans from different cultural, ethnic, or racial backgrounds.

The Process
1. Prior to the interview students identify topics of interest, and do some preliminary research on the topic they're going to discuss.
2. Students identify individuals to interview, contact these individuals to arrange an interview, giving the purpose, time, and place.
3. Working in groups, students prepare some questions for the interview and review with the class the questions they've chosen.
4. Students and the teacher than prepare for the interview. Questions should be simple, relevant, and varied. Procedures for interviewing should be reviewed with the class (let the respondent do the talking, don't interrupt a story, etc.).
5. During the interview, students take notes or record (audio or video) the data.
6. Following the interview, students transcribe their notes or recorded data to prepare material for publication or oral presentation.
7. Students then interpret and edit materials, verify dates, and obtain written release from respondent for "publication" to the whole class.

Working With a Partner in the Art Museum

In an art museum, students might focus on a few paintings or pieces of sculpture. Have students make up a question or two about some aspect of the art they wish to explore further—and respond to five or six questions from the list in a notebook or writing pad they take with them.

Possible Questions for Reflection

- Compare and contrast technology and art as vehicles for viewing the past, present, or future differently.
- How is the visual put together?
- How are images used to communicate?
- How did the creator of the visual image expect the viewer to actively engage the image? Is content more important than form?
- How does your social background affect how you receive (or construct) the message?
- Visuals are authored in much the way print communication is authored. How does the author of a picture or piece of sculpture manipulate the viewer through such things as point of view, size, distortion, or lighting?

- What are the largest or smallest artistic elements of the work?
- What is the main idea, mood, feeling, or intent conveyed by the image?
- When you close your eyes and think about the visual, what pictures do you see? What sounds do you hear? Does in remind you of anything—a book, a dream, TV, something from your life?
- How successful was the visual in making use of the medium?
- How successful is the sculpture or image? Does it have validity? Is it effective? What is your response to it?
- Where did the visual maker place important ideas?
- How do combinations or organization of elements contribute to an overall mood?
- Does the image tell us about big ideas such as courage, freedom, war, and so on.
- Determine the nature of the image through its style, period, school, and culture. How does it fit in with the history of art?
- What does the work say about present conflicts concerning art standards, multiculturalism and American culture?
- Estimate the esthetic value of the sculpture or image as it relates to others
- How did the work make you feel inside?
- Was the artistic work easy or hard to understand?
- Why do you think it was made: What would you like to change about it?

Strategies for Change

Active collaboration around a thematic approach requires a depth of planning, a redefinition of testing, and cooperative classroom management skills (Albert, 1990). Cooperative learning values differences of abilities, talents, and background knowledge. Within a cooperative learning classroom many conventionally defined "disabilities" integrate naturally into the heterogeneity of expected and anticipated differences among all students.

Organizing an interdisciplinary lesson around a theme can excite and motivate all students to actively carry out projects and tasks in their group. "Disabilities" and "differences" come to constitute part of the fabric of diversity that is celebrated and cherished within cooperative groups. In such an educational climate, no individual is singled out as being difficult and no one student presents an insurmountable challenge to the teacher when it comes to accommodating a student with special needs.

In a cooperative learning classroom, no student needs to be stereotyped by others when they realize that there are many and varied *differences* among students. It is easier for the student with special needs to fit in. For some pupils differences may in fact constitute an *disability,* defined as the inability to do a certain life or school-related task. Such a difference, however, need not constitute a handicap, as cooperative learning is a joint enterprise. Some may have a disability or special talent, but all have information and skills to contribute to the learning of others (Mercer & Mercer, 1985).

The central question is, how do individual classroom teachers, already overwhelmed with tasks, find ways to adapt collaborative techniques, plan thematically, and modify approaches for successfully accommodating all students within their classrooms? The problem is much broader than adapting techniques or modifying current methods. It involves rethinking the structure of the curriculum and seeking different approaches for teaching all students in a way that builds on their unique human qualities.

REFERENCES

Albert, L. (1990). *Cooperative discipline*. Circle Pines, MN: American Guidance Service.

Carnegie Foundation for the Advancement of Teaching. (1988). *The condition of teaching: A state-by-state analysis*. Princeton, NJ: Princeton University Press.

The College Board. (1985). *Academic preparation in the arts: Teaching for transition from high school to college*. New York: Author.

Csikszentmihalyi, M., & Csikszentmihalyi, I. (1988). *Optimal experience: Psychological studies*. New York: Cambridge University Press.

Dill, D. (1990). *What teachers need to know*. San Francisco, CA: Jossey-Bass.

Fraser, J.T. (1990). *Of time, passion and knowledge*. Princeton, NJ: Princeton University Press.

Gage, N.L., & Berliner, D. (1990). Nurturing the critical, practical, and artistic thinking of teachers. *Phi Delta Kappan, 71*(3), 212-14.

Jacobs, H. (1989). *Interdisciplinary curriculum: Design and implementation*. Alexandria, VA: Association for Supervision and Curriculum Development.

Maeroff, G. (1988). *The empowerment of teachers*. New York: Teachers College Press.

Mercer, C.D., & Mercer, A.R. (1985). *Teaching students with learning problems*. Columbus, OH: Merrill.

Middleton, K. (1990). *Into adolescence: Communicating emotions*. Santa Cruz, CA: ETR Associates/Network Publications.

Richardson, R., & Skinner, E. (1990). *Achieving access and quality*. New York: Macmillan.

Rogoff, B. (1990). *Apprentices in thinking: Children's guided participation in culture*. New York: Oxford University Press.

Sharan, S. (1990). *Cooperative learning: Theory and research*. Westport, CT: Bergin & Garvey and Praeger Publishing.

Sigley, M., & Anderson, J. (1990). *The transfer of cognitive skill*. Cambridge, MA: Harvard University Press.

Wlodkowski, R., & Jaynes, J. (1990). *Eager to learn*. San Francisco, CA: Jossey-Bass Publishers.

8

NEW ASSUMPTIONS, NEW MODELS, NEW PROCESSES

To link students with today's literacy-intensive world requires reaching beyond academic programs to gain a better feel for contemporary cultural conditions. As schools grapple with infusing multicultural concerns into the school reform process, it's important to remember the ways in which many racial, ethnic, and cultural groups have transformed American culture. A curriculum of *inclusion* can help the classroom reflect diverse social realities while connecting with a common national culture.

As public schools strive to create a civic community that is both expansive and inclusive, it is important to recognize that we are now in the midst of a transition from an industrial society to an "information-age" society. This requires new conceptual models and new ways of thinking. Two of the central features of the information age society are collaboration and communication. Basic paradigms for both must serve industry, civic culture, and education.

There are many intriguing assumptions suggested by the new collaboration communications model. These new concepts will serve to "shake the foundations" of much of what we have believed in the past to be important and essential to the process of schooling. The following list suggests but a few:

1. Learning is an active, very social process. People of different generations and cultures need to be involved with others. With fewer people coming into the workforce, *everyone* will be needed.
2. Learning is a very active mental process. The mind is always working, always learning. Critical and creative thinking skills help students generalize by adding information beyond what is given.

3. The prior experience of a student is an important ingredient of any learning situation.
4. The student must be a very active, self-initiating participant in the learning process.
5. Students need to verbalize their experiences and their new learnings on their own (language and conceptual) terms. Developing metaphors and analogies can assist with extending thinking and language.
6. Students are excellent teachers. They can teach each other. They can learn as much from their peers as from teachers.
7. The "things" to be learned are not really as compartmentalized as current curriculum fields may suggest. Everything is related and interrelated. Students need to discover these relationships. The relationships that students come up with may be different than the ones that teachers have because of differences in levels of past experiences and cognitive maturity.
8. Students are tremendously curious. They have a tremendous need to learn, to become competent.
9. Students enjoy and profit tremendously from working together and thereby learning together.
10. With proper development, students can become very responsible for managing their own learning opportunities.

All of these assumptions, coupled with cooperative learning, will lead to very different styles of teaching for the teacher. Interaction and information flow are major characteristics of the teaching/learning style. The "richer" the interaction, the more productive the learning. As students and teachers collaboratively undertake projects, they become joint learning ventures. Success (or grades) is not determined by achieving the highest score on a test. Rather it is determined by how well the learning project is accomplished and how well the various members of the learning "team" have interacted and worked together.

Cooperative problem finding is one of the most important skills for the learner (Holmes Group, 1988). This involves the ability to look at specific events and decide which ones are worthy of further analysis, a socially useful skill that we squander at our own risk. Working together, all children in the classroom can move from absorbing facts to thinking of solutions to the problems, and, ultimately, to deciding which problems are most urgent to solve.

Seeking New Instructional Models: Using Collaboration and Literature To Connect Subjects

The leap from the familiar, competitive (stimulus–response), production-control model of schooling to a communication cooperative model can seem enormous. To consider a change of such magnitude can seem threatening and unnerving for some. How then can we best make the transition and the instructional adjustments?

One way is to realize the similarities between how the teaching process is now organized and how it would be using cooperative learning strategies. There is considerable structure, motivation, and individual freedom within cooperative learning. Trusting peers and valuing diverse contributions is central to developing a collaborative framework. Also, cooperative learning can be applied within any curriculum area as conventionally defined by existing curriculum guides or content area textbooks. Thus, a teacher can adapt this model quite easily without make drastic changes to the knowledge or skill objectives that are already specified for a course. The textbook does not have to be their own out but, rather, extended to include active learning procedures where student groups are involved in searching out information, clarifying connections, explaining concepts, working on cooperative projects, solving problems, and "finding out"—rather than "filling in."

When using cooperative learnings strategies, teachers stress the importance of experiential and world knowledge in learning. New material, information, knowledge, and skills are explored, interpreted, and extended on the basis of what the students already know. This integration is suggested by the recent development of the "whole language" approach to learning. Whole language is a shorthand way of referring to a set of beliefs about teaching and learning. In this approach students might read real literature about historical events or scientific breakthroughs. Many teachers use the whole language approach as a way to connect various subjects and get students to share ideas.

Cooperative learning lends itself to integrating a number of subject matter areas while recognizing the importance of the students' prior knowledge for creating new knowledge. A basic assumption is that students are not passive recipients of information or skills. Therefore they are encouraged to actively engage their worlds in order to learn and construct their own meanings (Timar & Kirp, 1988). Students do this by expressing their ideas through talking, writing, problem solving, and artistic expression. Teachers do their share by modeling these processes and developing teaching styles that are more active and engaging.

The Central Role of Professional Educators

It is a violation of the idea of a liberal imagination to suggest that sincere teaching could proceed without authentic scholars as if these apparently opposing selves were not reconcilable as mutual influences.
—Joan Baum

There is general agreement that American schools don't have a choice about changing—and that educators must be intimately involved in the effort (Schlechty, 1990). It's too late for tinkering around the edges. Our educational systems will get—like it or not—massive, systematic restructuring. Leadership must be bold and occasionally wrong to move things along. At the school site level, there will be wider participation by all faculty in developing curriculum and setting school policy (Sergiovanni, 1990). As things now stand, teachers just don't have time to plan new curricula, collaborate with peers, take part in scholarly activities, or attend in-service programs to keep their skills at a high level. Teachers need time and incentives for becoming involved in taking on these new responsibilities. New teachers, for example, need thorough orientation programs and mentors who are successful in a multicultural environment. Their educational preparation hasn't prepared them to help their students live their lives in a racially and culturally diverse nation.

Consciously thinking about and affirming a new set of education a values means recognizing the importance of diversity, valuing students' prior knowledge, and actively engaging student groups in the learning process. As classrooms are organized for cooperative learning, peers take responsibility for some of the teaching—allowing the power of the teacher to be multiplied (Barth, 1990). Many are already in the process of making the transition from a system where the teacher is viewed as an external operator of the system, to a model of cooperation where the teacher is a facilitator or academic choreographer.

Collaboration With Colleagues At Many Educational Levels

Inherent in the concept of the cooperative model is the notion of teacher-to-teacher assistance. The interactive nature of the cooperative model itself enhances the possibility of working closely, with other teachers and support professionals. In some schools this may mean a revamping of traditional departmental arrangements to facilitate interdisciplinary coordination. For example, teachers with strengths in social science topics may find themselves planning and working with teachers whose strengths are in music, science or language. Similarly, classroom teachers may find themselves working jointly with special education teachers. When they work as a professional team, teachers can plan and teach together to meet the academic and equity needs of students.

Making sure that teachers have collaborative opportunities is central involving them in a larger role, such as shaping their profession or changing school organizational patterns (Orlich, 1989). This involves urging universities to improve their connection to the schools. All colleges should establish partnerships with nearby schools and involve their faculty members with public schools and teachers. Additionally, colleges in many states will be asked to play an even broader role in the school reform process by improving their teacher-education programs and raising the status and stature of such programs in the university hierarchy.

The curriculum of our schools must be based on the knowledge and practices that have been determined by professionals)—competent teachers and scholars (Holmes, Leithwood, & Musella, 1989). Collaboration between professional educators allows classroom teachers to broaden their teaching techniques and reach a wider range of today's students.

Fueling the National Imagination

Educational consciousness raising has brought home the notion that the future is connected to quality schools. It is now generally agreed that we need educational changes—and we need big ones. The best way to pursue this reformation isn't through hard and fast dictums from above, but through debate and an effort to explore what reliable data shows us to work. The exact dimensions will have to be hammered out by educators as they go along. Teachers will be major decision makers in the school improvement process, because they know more than legislators and businessmen about how schools should be structured and what good programs should look like.

American leaders have set a series of educational goals for the year 2000:

- "All children will start school ready to learn."
- "The graduation rate (high school) will be no less than 90%."
- "U.S. students will be first in the world in literacy, mathematics, and scientific achievement."
- "Every adult will be literate and possess knowledge and skills to compete globally" (National Governor's Association, 1990).

It has proven wiser politically to set goals than to start programs. National objectives can be powerful expressions of high aspirations and purpose and goal structures can help move people to action. But adequate national means and social energy must be coupled with these goals if they are to be implemented. Even the best of intentions are not enough to defeat overwhelming social and educational ills. There must be a serious sustained social commitment to keep disillusionment from setting in. Educators, for their part, are already exploring how they can carry their share of the burden.

Restructuring schools means changing the basic human relationships, as well as the educational community. Active team learning, equity, linking disciplines, creative thinking skills, and educational technology will all be part of the major curriculum initiatives in the 1990s. But it's the human element that will make the difference. To change the basic structure of schooling requires well-educated teachers with vision and stamina. Hiring and retaining people who are excited about teaching and learning can help change the school culture and have a real impact on whether or not a child learns (Elmore, 1990).

One of the major challenges in school reform is figuring out how to harness enough enlightened social energy and initiative to fuel the national imagination. Today many of our young people don't sell their dreams, they have them siphoned off by the country's social and educational disinvestment in their future. Failure to act on educational change now means continuing to watch students drift through (or out of) public schools as they daily experience the diminishment of the American dream. Many adults are skeptical of educational reform and doubt its potential for empowering and improving the lives of children. Let's prove them wrong.

What is missed most isn't something that's gone, but possibilities that will never happen.
—Margaret Atwood

REFERENCES

Barth, R. (1990). *Improving schools from within*. San Francisco: Jossey-Bass.

Elmore, R. (1990). *Restructuring schools*. San Francisco: Jossey-Bass.

Holmes, M., Leithwood, K., & Musella, D. (1989). *Educational policy for effective schools*. New York: Teachers College Press.

Holmes Group. (1988). *Forum, 3*(1), 2-6.

National Governor's Association Report. (1990). *Educating America: State strategies for 1990: Achieving education goals*. Washington, DC: U.S. Government Printing Office.

Orlich, D. (1989). *Staff development: Enhancing human potential*. Needham Heights, MA: Allyn and Bacon.

Schlechty, P. (1990). *Schools for the 21st century*. San Francisco: Jossey Bass.

Sergiovanni, T. J. (1990). *Value-added leadership: How to get extraordinary performance in schools*. New York: Harcourt Brace Jovanovich.

Timar, T., & Kirp, D. (1988). *Managing educational excellence*. Philadelphia: Falmer.

Author Index

Subject Index